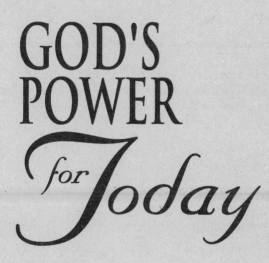

GOD'S
POWER
for Today

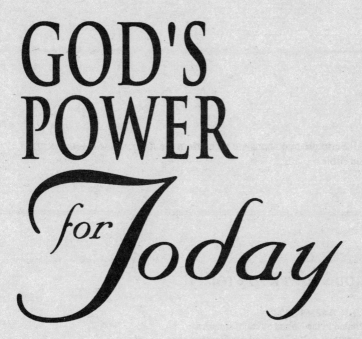

GOD'S POWER for Today

ANDREW MURRAY

🅦 Whitaker House

All Scripture quotations are taken from the *King James Version* (KJV) of the Bible.

GOD'S POWER FOR TODAY

ISBN: 0-88368-300-8
Printed in the United States of America
Copyright © 1997 by Whitaker House

Whitaker House
30 Hunt Valley Circle
New Kensington, PA 15068

Library of Congress Cataloging-in-Publication Data

Murray, Andrew, 1828–1917.
    God's power for today / by Andrew Murray.
        p.   cm.
    ISBN 0-88368-300-8 (trade paper)
    1. Devotional calendars. 2. Christian life. I. Title.
BV4811.G84 1997
242'.2—dc21   97-31582

1 2 3 4 5 6 7 8 9 10 11 12 13 / 06 05 04 03 02 01 00 99 98 97

Contents

January

January

1

When you get a promise from God, it is worth just as much as a fulfillment. You only need to honor Him by trusting the promise and obeying Him. God knows about any preparation that you still need. If there is anything that you need to understand, He will lead you to understand it, if you count on Him to do this. Do not look to what others say or to what you think and understand. Look to God, and expect God to do something.

The true taking away of sin is this: if the light comes in, the darkness is expelled. It is the presence of Jesus indwelling in us by the Holy Spirit that can make us holy. The Spirit did everything on the Day of Pentecost and afterwards. It was the Spirit who gave the boldness, the wisdom, the message, and the converting power.

2

Let everyone who longs for the blessing of the Spirit take these four little sayings as steps: I must be filled; I may be filled; I would be filled; I will be filled.

What is obedience? It is giving up my will to the will of another. Christ said, *"Not my will, but thine, be done"* (Luke 22:42). Jesus gave up His life to God, and by this He taught us that the only thing that life is worth living for is to give it back to God, even unto death.

Christ never could have ascended to sit upon the throne, never could have accomplished His work of preparing the kingdom so that He could give it to the Father, if He had not begun by giving up Himself and letting God do all.

3

The throne in heaven is not the throne of the Lamb of God alone; it is the throne of God and the Lamb. Jesus went to share the throne with the Father; the Father was always the first and Jesus the second.

There are two spirits on earth. Paul said, *"We have received, not the spirit of the world, but the spirit which is of God"* (1 Cor. 2:12). This is the great need in every Christian worker: the spirit of the world going out, and the Spirit of God coming in to take possession of the inner life and of the whole being. Oh, what fellowship! The Holy Spirit in heaven doing part of the work, man on earth doing the other part. After the ordination of the men on earth, it is written in God's inspired Word that they were sent forth by the Holy Spirit.

4

Jesus said to Peter, "Deny yourself," and again, *"Thou shalt deny me"* (Matt. 26:34). There is no choice for us; we must either deny self or deny Christ. Deliverance from the self-life means to be a vessel overflowing with love to everybody all day.

It is when the individual workers are blessed that the work will prosper and the body of Christ will be in health and strength.

Before God took His Son up to heaven, He let Him live here on earth, so that through the example of His life I might have a complete representation of what my God wanted me to be and was willing to make me. How am I to live this life of absolute surrender? The Father points to the beloved Son and says, *"This is my beloved Son, in whom I am well pleased"* (Matt. 3:17). Hear Him, follow Him, live like Him, and let Christ be the rule of your life.

5

If a vessel that ought to be whole is cracked into many pieces, it cannot be filled. You can take one part of it and possibly dip out a little water, but if you want the vessel full, the vessel must be whole. This is true of Christ's church. If there is one thing we have to pray for, it is this: Lord, melt us together into one by the power of the Holy Spirit.

The will of the creature is nothing but an empty vessel in which the power of God is to be made manifest.

God does not work by His Spirit as He works by a blind force in nature. He leads His people on as reasonable, intelligent beings. Therefore, when we have come to the end of self, to the conviction that, though we have been striving to obey the law, we have failed, then He shows us that in the Holy Spirit we have the power of obedience, victory, and real holiness.

6

When a question is asked, an answer is expected. Alas, how many Christians are content with the question: *"O wretched man that I am! who shall deliver me from the body of this death?"* (Rom. 7:24). Instead of saying, *"I thank God through Jesus Christ our Lord"* (v. 25), they are forever repeating the question without the answer.

God has called the church of Christ to live in the power of the Holy Spirit, and the church is living for the most part in the power of human flesh and of will and energy and effort apart from the Spirit of God. If the church will acknowledge that the Holy Spirit is her strength and her help, will give up everything and wait upon God to be filled with the Spirit, her days of beauty and gladness will return, and we will see the glory of God revealed among us.

7

I have often been asked by young Christians, "Why is it that I fail so? I did so solemnly vow with my whole heart and did desire to serve God; why have I failed?" You are trying to do in your own strength what Christ alone can do in you. You were trusting in yourself, or you would not have failed. If you had trusted Christ, He could not fail. We find the Christian life so difficult because we seek God's blessing while we live in our own will. We make our own plans and choose our own work, and then we ask Him to give us His blessing.

You cannot work out God's will, but His Holy Spirit can. Until the church, until believers grasp this and cease trying by human effort to do God's will and wait upon the Holy Spirit to come with all His omnipotent and enabling power, the church will never be what God wants her to be and what God is willing to make of her.

8

You may have ten hours of hard work daily, during which your brain has to be occupied with temporal things. God orders it so. But abiding in Jesus is the work of the heart, not of the brain. The heart clings to and rests in Jesus, a work in which the Holy Spirit links us to Jesus. Deeper down than the brain, deep down in the inner life, you can abide in Christ so that every moment that you are free the consciousness will come: Blessed Jesus, I am still in You.

Do not confuse work and fruit. There may be a good deal of work for Christians that is not the fruit of the Heavenly Vine. Do not seek for work only. Fruit-bearing means the very life and power and spirit and love within the heart of the Son of God, the Heavenly Vine Himself, coming into your heart and mine.

9

God has given us an incorruptible inheritance, reserved in heaven for us, who are kept by the power of God (1 Pet. 1:4–5). My God is keeping the inheritance for me and keeping me for the inheritance. The same power, the same love, the same God is doing the double work.

Let us say that I have borrowed a watch from a friend, and I break it. The hands are broken, the face is defaced, and some of the wheels and springs are spoiled. If I were to take it back in that condition, my friend would say, "I did not want you to keep my watch so that you would bring me back only the shell of the watch. I expected you to keep it together." In the same way, God does not want to keep us in a general way, so that we will just get into heaven, but the keeping power and love of God apply to every part of our being.

10

The altar sanctifies the gift. Christ is not only the Priest and the Victim, but the Living Christ is Himself the Altar. Though I am all unworthy and all feeble, the altar sanctifies the gift. Through being in Jesus and resting on Him, my God accepts my feebleness, and I am pleasing in His sight.

Picture a clock. If I see that the hands stand still and point wrongly, and that the clock is slow or fast, I say that there is something inside the clock that is not right. Disposition or character is like the revelation that the clock gives of what is within. It is a proof of whether the love of Christ is filling the heart.

11

Does it cost the lamb any trouble to be gentle? No, it is its nature. Why does it not trouble a wolf to be cruel and to put its fangs into the poor lamb? Because that is its nature. How can I learn to love? I can never learn to love until the Spirit of God fills my heart with God's love.

There is a difference between the power of the Spirit as a gift and the power of the Spirit for the

gra...
of th...
measu...
holines...

On the... Day of Pente... and Peter w... a change... Christ, "You c... never... *thee'* (Matt. 16:...). He did... what it was to p... through... hear him say, *"If...* *Christ, happy are y... God resteth upon you...* (1 Pet. 4:14)... ...s not the old Peter, but the very... ...reathing and speaking within him.

Suppose that when a painter came into his studio to paint an unfinished picture, the canvas always moved to some other part of the room. Of course the painter could not paint. Suppose the canvas would say, "O painter, I will be still; come and paint your beautiful picture." Then the painter would come and do it. Say to God, "You are the wondrous artist. I am still. I trust Your power." God will then work wonders with you. God never works anything but wonders.

13

Your religious life is to be a proof every day that God works things that are impossible. Your religious life is to be a series of impossibilities made possible and actual by God's almighty power. I do not want idle talk of God's power, but I want—let me say this with reverence—the whole of God's omnipotence to keep me right and make me live like a Christian.

ur work comes between
ad thought that the bearing
arate the branch from the vine.
ecause we have looked on our work as
ther than the branch bearing fruit.

thank God for the interest that He is awaken-
g in foreign missions, in drunkards, in the poor
outcast. However, considering the middle classes,
the richer and higher classes, is there no power in
your duty to take the Gospel to them boldly?

14

All that Christ is and has is not in Himself, but
from the Father. Before He ever tells believers about
abiding in Him or bearing fruit, Christ turns their
eyes heavenward to the Father who is watching over
them and working in them. The great lack of the
Christian life is that even when we trust Christ, we
leave God out of the picture. Christ came to bring us
to God. Christ lived the life of a man exactly as we
have to live it. Christ, the Vine, points to God, the
Divine Cultivator.

15

Think of the vine first. The branch has only one
objective for which it exists, one purpose to which it
is entirely given up: to bear the fruit the vine wishes
to bring forth. And so the believer has only one reason for his being a branch, only one reason for his
existence on earth: so that the Heavenly Vine may
bring forth His fruit through him. Second, the
branch is exactly like the vine in every aspect: the
same nature, the same life, the same place, the same

work. In all this, they are inseparably one. And so the believer needs to know that he is a partaker of the divine nature and has the very nature and spirit of Christ in him, and that his one calling is to yield himself to a perfect conformity to Christ. Third, the vine has its stores of life and sap and strength, not for itself, but for the branches. The branches have nothing but what the vine provides and imparts. The branch only has to yield itself and receive. This truth leads to the blessed rest of faith and the true secret of growth and strength: *"I can do all things through Christ which strengtheneth me"* (Phil. 4:13).

16

Before we begin to think of fruit or branches, let us have our hearts filled with this knowledge: as glorious as the Vine is, so is the Cultivator. As high and holy as our calling is, so mighty and loving is the God who will work it all out. As truly as the Cultivator made the Vine what it was to be, so will He make each branch what it is to be. Many Christians think their own salvation is the first thing, their worldly lives the second, and then what is left of time and interest is to be devoted to fruit-bearing and the saving of men. In most cases, very little time or interest can be found. The one condition of my abiding and growing strong is that I bear the fruit of the Heavenly Vine for dying men to eat and live.

17

As churches and individuals, we are in danger of nothing as much as self-contentment. The secret spirit of Laodicea—we are rich and increased in goods and have need of nothing (Rev. 3:14–17)—may prevail where not suspected. The divine warning, *"wretched, and miserable, and poor"* (v. 17), finds little response where it is most needed. Let us not rest contentedly with the thought that we are taking an equal share with others in the work or that men are satisfied with our efforts. Let our only desire be to know whether we are bearing all the fruit Christ is willing to give through us as living branches, in close and living union with Himself.

18

What a solemn, precious lesson. The cleansing of the Cultivator does not refer to sin only. It refers also to our own religious activity, as it is developed in the very act of bearing fruit. In working for God, our natural gifts of wisdom, eloquence, influence, or zeal are always in danger of being unduly developed and then trusted in. So, after each season of work, God has to bring us to the end of ourselves, to the consciousness of the helplessness and the danger of all that is of man, so that we can feel that we are nothing. All that is to be left of us is just enough to receive the power of the life-giving sap of the Holy Spirit. What comes from man must be reduced to its very lowest measure. All that is inconsistent with the most entire devotion to Christ's service must be removed. The more perfect the cleansing and cutting away of all that is of self, the more intense the concentration can be of our whole being to be entirely at the disposal of the Spirit.

19

Many believers pray and long very earnestly for the filling of the Spirit and the indwelling of Christ, and they wonder why they do not make more progress. The reason is often this: the *"I in you"* cannot come because the *"Abide in me"* (John 15:4) is not maintained. *"There is one body, and one Spirit"* (Eph. 4:4). Before the Spirit can fill, a body must be prepared. The graft must have grown into the stem and be abiding in it before the sap can flow through to bring forth fruit. As we follow Christ in lowly obedience—denying ourselves and forsaking the world, even in external things, and seeking to be conformable to Him, even in the body—as we thus seek to abide in Him, we will be able to receive and enjoy the *"I in you."* The work ordained for us, *"Abide in me,"* will prepare us for the work undertaken by Him, *"I in you."*

The vision of Christ is an irresistible attraction; it draws and holds us like a magnet. Always listen to the living Christ still speaking to you and waiting to show you the meaning and power of His word: *"I am the vine"* (John 15:5). So it sometimes happens that souls who have never been especially occupied with the thought of abiding, are abiding all the time, because they are occupied with Christ.

20

Have you ever noticed the difference in the Christian life between work and fruit? A machine can do work; only life can bear fruit. A law can compel work; only love can spontaneously bring forth fruit. Work implies effort and labor; the essential idea of fruit is that it is the silent, natural, restful produce of our inner lives. The connection between work and fruit is, perhaps, best seen in the expression, *"fruitful in every good work"* (Col.

1:10). It is only when good works come as the fruit of the indwelling Spirit that they are acceptable to God. Under the compulsion of law and conscience, or the influence of inclination and zeal, men may be most diligent in good works and yet find that they have little spiritual result. Their works are man's effort instead of being the fruit of the Spirit—the restful, natural outcome of the Spirit's operation within us.

21

A deep conviction of the truth of this passage, *"Except ye abide in me...ye can do nothing"* (John 15:4–5), lies at the very root of a strong spiritual life. As much as I created myself, as much as I could raise a man from the dead, can I give myself the divine life and maintain or increase it. Every motion is the work of God through Christ and His Spirit. As a man believes this, he will take up that position of entire and continual dependence that is the very essence of the life of faith. His whole heart says "Amen" to the passage, *"Ye can do nothing."* And because he does so, he can also say, *"I can do all things through Christ which strengtheneth me"* (Phil. 4:13).

22

Only by praying much can we fulfill our calling to bear much fruit. All the treasures men around us need are hidden in Christ. In Him all God's children are blessed with all spiritual blessings (Eph. 1:3). He is full of grace and truth. But prayer, much prayer, strong believing prayer, is needed to bring these blessings down. We cannot take hold of the promise in John 15:7, *"If ye abide in me, and my words abide in you, ye shall ask what ye will, and it shall be done unto you,"* without a life given up for men.

23

There have always been a smaller number of God's people who have sought to serve Him with their whole hearts, while the majority have been content with a very small measure of the knowledge of His grace and will. And what is the difference between this smaller inner circle and the many who do not seek admission to it? We find it in the following: much fruit. With many Christians, the thought of personal safety, which at their first awakening was a legitimate one, remains the one aim of their religion to the end. The idea of service and fruit is always a secondary and very subordinate one. We see these two classes of disciples everywhere in God's Word. Let our desire be nothing less than perfect cleansing, unbroken abiding, closest communion, abundant fruitfulness—true branches of the True Vine.

24

Some have told of a wonderful change by which their lives of continual failure and stumbling had been changed into a very blessed experience of being kept, strengthened, and made exceedingly glad. If you asked them how this great blessing came to them, many would tell you it was simply that they were led to believe that this abiding in Christ's love was meant to be a reality and that they were made willing to give up everything for it and then enabled to trust Christ to make it true to them. The feebleness of our Christian life is that we do not take time to believe that this divine Love really does delight in us and will possess and work all through us. We do not take time to look at the Vine bearing the branch so entirely, working all in it so completely. We strive to do for ourselves what Christ alone can, what Christ so lovingly longs to, do for us.

25

Let me say to all, so that you may gladly believe fully: Cherish every whisper of the conscience and of the Spirit who convinces you of sin. Whatever it is— a hasty temper, a sharp word, an unloving or impatient thought, anything of selfishness or self-will— cherish that which condemns it in you, as part of the schooling to bring you to Christ and the full possession of His salvation.

Obedience is the blessed link between what God has already worked in us and what He waits to work.

26

God's will is the very center of His divine perfection. As revealed in His commandments, it opens up the way for the creature to grow into the likeness of the Creator. In accepting and doing His will, I rise into fellowship with Him. This is why the Son, when coming into the world, said, *"I come to do thy will, O God"* (Heb. 10:9). This was the place, and this would be the blessedness of the creature. This was what man had lost in the Fall. This was what Christ came to restore. This is what, as the Heavenly Vine, He asks of us and imparts to us, that even as He, by keeping His Father's commandments, abided in His love, we should keep His commandments and abide in His love.

27

The Word is God's pruning knife, *"sharper than any twoedged sword, piercing even to the dividing asunder of soul and spirit...and is a discerner of the thoughts and intents of the heart"* (Heb. 4:12). Affliction only becomes a blessing when it leads to the Word; the lack of this heart-cleansing through the Word is the reason why affliction is so often unsanctified. Jesus says, *"Ye are clean through the word which I have spoken unto you"* (John 15:3).

It is as the soul gives up its own thoughts and men's thoughts of what religion is, and yields itself heartily, humbly, and patiently to the teaching of the Word by the Spirit, that the Father will do His blessed work of pruning and cleansing away all of nature and self that mixes with our work and hinders His Spirit. If anyone asks, "How can I be a happy Christian?" our Lord's answer is very simple: *"'These things* [about the Vine and the branches] *I have spoken unto you, that in me ye might have peace....that* [you] *might have my joy fulfilled in* [yourselves]' (John 16:33; 17:13). You cannot have My joy without My life. Abide in Me and let Me abide in you (John 15:4), and My joy will be in you." All healthy life is a thing of joy and beauty. Live the branch life undividedly, and you will have His joy in full measure.

28

To many Christians, the thought of a life wholly abiding in Christ is one of strain and painful effort. The strain and effort come only as long as we do not yield ourselves unreservedly to the life of Christ in us. The very first words of the parable are not yet opened up to them: *"I am the true vine"* (John 15:1). "I undertake all and provide for all. I ask nothing of the branch except that it should yield wholly to Me and allow Me to do all. I engage to make and keep the branch all that it ought to be."

29

As we know His dying love, we will joyfully obey its commands; as we obey the commands, we will know the love more fully. The imperative necessity of obedience, doing all that Christ commands us, does not have the place in our Christian teaching and living that Christ meant it to have. We have given a far higher place to privilege than to duty. We have not considered implicit obedience as a condition of true discipleship. The secret thought that it is impossible to do the things He commands us and that therefore it cannot be expected of us—a subtle and unconscious feeling that sinning is a necessity—has frequently robbed both precepts and promises of their power. Let us take Christ's words as most literally true and make nothing less the law of our life: *"Ye are my friends, if ye do whatsoever I command you"* (John 15:14).

30

Throughout Scripture this is the great object of the teaching of election: *"Predestinate[d] to be conformed to the image of his Son"* (Rom. 8:29), to be branches in the image and likeness of the Vine. *"Chosen...that we should be holy"* (Eph. 1:4). *"Chosen...to salvation through sanctification of the Spirit"* (2 Thess. 2:13). *"Elect...through sanctification of the Spirit, unto obedience"* (1 Pet. 1:2). In

J... ...Christ...
cl... ...to be T...
fr... on earth and ...
pr...

arou... you? It is ...
your... strength or all ...
secur... this. All ...
God a...d His power, first ...
living ...the truly ...of abiding in ...
close a...d unbroken ...with Christ. It is the
branch ...that abides in Him that brings forth much
fruit, fr...t that will abide.

It is ...because we so little live the true branch life,
because ...so little love ...in the Vine to
abide in ... ...ly, that we feel so little constrained to much prayer and so little confident that
we will be heard. So then, we do not know how to
use His name as the key to God's storehouse. The
power of direct access to the Father for men, the liberty of intercession, claiming and receiving blessing
for them in faith, is the highest exercise of our union
with Christ. Let all who would truly and fully be
branches give themselves to the work of intercession. It is the one great work of Christ, the Vine in
heaven, the source of power for all His work. Make it
your one great work as a branch. It will be the power
of all your work.

John 15:16, Christ...
...choosing us to be His...
...fruit on earth, and have...
...ayer.

26

Are you leaving your trust for st...
...behind you? It is not your preaching or...
...your strength of will or power to influence...
...secure this. All depends on having your life in...
...God and His power. And that again depends on your...
...of the truly branchlike life of abiding, in very...
...deed and unbroken fellowship with Christ. It is the...
...branch that abides in Him that brings forth much...
...fruit, fruit that will abide.

...is because we so little live the true branch life...
...because we so little lose ourselves in Christ, that...
...abide in Him entirely, that we feel so little the...
...constraining power of Christ's...

February

February

1

As long as we expect God to do for us what we ask or think, we limit Him. When we believe that as high as the heavens are above the earth, His thoughts are above our thoughts (Isa. 55:9), and when we wait on Him as God to do unto us according to His word, as He means, we will live the truly supernatural, heavenly life the Holy Spirit can work in us: the true Christ life.

2

We all know the need of time for our meals each day. If we are to live through Jesus, we must thoroughly take in and assimilate that heavenly food the Father has given us in His life. My fellow believer, if you want to learn to abide in Jesus, take time each day to put yourself into living contact with the living Jesus and to yield yourself distinctly and consciously to His blessed influence. If you do this, you will give Him the opportunity to take hold of you, to draw you up and keep you safe in His almighty life.

3

Jesus gives rest in Himself: the rest of pardon and acceptance, the rest in His love. But, we know all that God bestows needs time to become fully our own. It must be held fast and appropriated and assimilated into our inmost being. Without this, not even Christ's giving can make it our very own in full experience and enjoyment.

4

Giving up one's whole life to Him, for Him alone to rule and order it; taking up His yoke and submitting to be led and taught, to learn of Him; abiding in Him, to be and do only what He wills—these are the conditions of discipleship without which there can be no thought of maintaining the rest that was bestowed on first coming to Christ. The Christian's rest is in Christ and not of the Christian. He does not give it apart from Himself, and so it is only in having Him that rest can really be kept and enjoyed.

5

Consecration and faith are the essential elements of the Christian life, the giving up all to Jesus, the receiving all from Jesus. They are implied in each other. They are united in one word: surrender.

Abiding in Him is not a work that we have to do as the condition for enjoying His salvation, but a consenting to let Him do all for us.

It was because Paul knew that the Mighty and the Faithful One had grasped him with the glorious purpose of making him one with Himself, that he did his utmost to grasp the glorious prize.

6

What loss the church is suffering because so few believers truly live as the heirs of the new covenant, in the true knowledge and enjoyment of its promises.

There is a twofold work of the Spirit: one in giving a holy disposition and character, the other in qualifying and empowering a man for work. The former must always come first. The promise that the disciples would receive the Holy Spirit for their service was very definitely given to those who had followed and loved Christ and had kept His commandments.

7

Salvation is nothing but love conquering and entering into us. We have just as much of salvation as we have of love. Full salvation is perfect love. There is no knowing God but by having life; the life working in us alone gives knowledge. And even so, if we would know the love, we must drink of its living stream. We must have it shed forth by the Holy Spirit in us.

8

As a prophet, Christ is our wisdom, revealing to us God and His love, with the nature and conditions of the salvation that love has prepared. As a priest, He is our righteousness, restoring us to a right relationship with God and securing to us His favor and friendship. As a king, He is our sanctification, forming and guiding us into the obedience to the Father's holy will. As these three offices work out God's purpose, the grand consummation will be reached, the complete deliverance from sin and all its effects will be accomplished, and ransomed humanity will regain all that it had ever lost!

9

The minister of the Spirit must especially see to it that he leads men to the Holy Spirit. Men may become too dependent on the preacher instead and may get their Scripture teaching secondhandedly. The new covenant is, *"They shall teach no more every man...his brother, saying, Know the LORD: for they shall all know me, from the least of them unto the greatest"* (Jer. 31:34). The minister of the Spirit points away from himself very definitely and perseveringly points to the Spirit. This is what John the Baptist did. Christ did the same. In His farewell discourse, He called His disciples to turn from His personal instruction to the inward teaching of the Holy Spirit.

10

The believer knows himself to be in the school of God. God is a Teacher who plans the whole course of study for each of His pupils with infinite wisdom and who delights to have them come daily for the lessons He has to give. All the believer asks is to feel himself constantly in God's hands and to follow His guidance, neither lagging behind nor going before.

11

In the service of our spiritual life, God has provided most bountifully for the sanctifying of our memory. The Holy Spirit is the memory of the new man. Blessed be God! It is as we see what Jesus is, and is to us, that the abiding in Him will become the natural and spontaneous result of our knowledge of Him.

12

Each blessed experience that we receive as a gift of God must at once be returned back to Him from whom it came. It should be returned in praise and love, in self-sacrifice and service, so that it can be restored to us again, fresh and beautiful with the bloom of heaven.

13

Christ's joy is ours whether we look backward and see the work He has done, or upward and see the reward He has in the Father's love that passes knowledge, or forward in the continual additions of joy as sinners are brought home.

14

What made the sick, the blind, and the needy in the Gospels so much more ready to believe than we are? There can be no strong faith without strong desire. Desire is the great motivating power in the universe. God's desire to save us moved Him to send His Son. Desire for salvation is the only thing that brings a sinner to Christ. Desire for God, fellowship with Him and His will, will make the Promised Land attractive. All indeed wish, in a way, to be better than they are, but few really *"hunger and thirst after righteousness"* (Matt. 5:6).

15

The heart that is occupied with its own plans and efforts for doing God's will, and with securing the blessing of abiding in Jesus, will fail continually. God can do His work perfectly only when the soul ceases from its work. He will do His work mightily in the soul that honors Him by expecting Him to work both *"to will and to do"* (Phil. 2:13).

16

Christ was the revelation of the Father on earth. Believers are the revelation of Christ on earth. They cannot be this unless there is perfect unity so that the world can know that He loves them and has sent them. But they can be the revelation of Christ since He loves them with infinite love that gives itself and all it has, if they abide in that love.

17

The secret of a life of close abiding will be seen to be simply this: As I give myself wholly to Christ, I find the power to take Him wholly for myself, and as I lose myself and all I have for Him, He takes me wholly for Himself and gives Himself wholly to me. Let a living faith in Christ working in you be the secret spring of all your work.

18

The believer who studies the life of Christ as the pattern and the promise of what his life may be, learns to understand how *"without me ye can do nothing"* (John 15:5), is but the forerunner of *"I can do all things through Christ which strengtheneth me"* (Phil. 4:13). We learn to glory in infirmities, to take pleasure in necessities and distresses for Christ's sake, because *"when I am weak, then am I strong"* (2 Cor. 12:10).

19

In the life of divine love, the emptying of self and the sacrifice of our will is the surest way to have all we can wish or will. Dependence, subjection, and self-sacrifice are for the Christian, as much as they are for Christ, the blessed path of life. As Christ lived through and in the Father, the believer can live in and through Christ.

20

To him who is really seeking to abide in Christ's love, the commands become no less precious than the promises. They are the revelation of the divine love, as much as the promises. They are blessed helpers in the path to a closer union with the Lord.

21

To the Christian, no sooner is the doing of God's will what Scripture and the Holy Spirit reveal it to be—the restoration to communion with God and conformity to Him—than he feels that there is no law more natural or more beautiful than this: Keeping Christ's commandments is the way to abide in Christ's love.

22

The weakest believer may be confident that, in asking to be kept from sin, to grow in holiness, and to bring forth much fruit, he may count on his petitions being fulfilled with divine power. The power is in Jesus. Jesus is ours with all His fullness. It is in us, His members, that the power is to work and to be made manifest.

23

The promise, *"Whatsoever ye shall ask in my name"* (John 14:13), may not be severed from the commandment, *"Whatsoever ye do...do all in the name of the Lord Jesus"* (Col. 3:17). If the name of Christ is to be wholly at my disposal, I must first put myself wholly at His disposal so that He has full and free command of me. It is the abiding in Christ that gives the right and power to use His name with confidence.

24

We have to be faithful each day for the one short day, and then long years and a long life will take care of themselves without the sense of their length or their weight ever being a burden. The single days do indeed make up the whole life, and the value of each single day depends on its influence on the whole life.

25

Abiding by faith in Christ, who is our sanctification, is the simple secret of a holy life. The measure of sanctification will depend on the measure of abiding in Him. As the soul learns to abide wholly in Christ, the following promise is increasingly fulfilled: *"The very God of peace sanctify you wholly"* (1 Thess. 5:23).

26

As our communion with Him becomes more intimate and intense, and as we let the Holy Spirit reveal Him to us in His heavenly glory, we realize how the life in us is the life of One who sits upon the throne of heaven. We feel the power of an endless life working in us. We taste the eternal life. We have the foretaste of the eternal glory.

27

Not only is what is given up to Christ received back again to become doubly our own, but the forsaking of all is followed by the receiving of all. We abide in Christ more fully as we forsake all and follow Him. As I count all things loss for His sake (Phil. 3:8), I am found in Him.

28

In Him you have a thousand times more given to you than you have lost. You see how God only took from you so that you might have room to take from Him what is so much better.

When you see affliction coming, meet it in Christ. When it has come, feel that you are more in Christ than in the affliction, for He is nearer to you than affliction ever can be. When it is passing, still abide in Him.

29

The objective of our daily lives must be to make an impression on others that is favorable to Jesus. When you look at the branch, you see at once the likeness to the Vine. We must live so that something of the holiness and the gentleness of Jesus may shine out in us. We must live to represent Him.

March

March

1

We have been redeemed to study the image of God in the Man, Christ Jesus. We need to yield and open our inmost being for that image to take possession and live in us, and then to go forth and let the heavenly likeness reflect itself and shine out in our lives among our fellowmen. Let this be what we live for.

2

The reason why we so often do not bless others is that we wish to address them as their superiors in grace or gifts, or at least as their equals. The love of Christ flowing into you will flow again from you and make it your greatest joy to follow His example in washing the feet of others.

3

The external and bodily life is the gate to the inner and spiritual life. Christ makes the salvation of the soul the first objective in His holy ministry of love. However, at the same time, He is seeking the way to hearts by the ready service of love in the little and common things of daily life.

4

Because my Surety is not someone outside of me, but One in whom I am and who is in me, I can then become like Him. He Himself lives in me. To follow His footsteps is a duty because it is a possibility, the natural result of the wonderful union between Head and members. I have to gaze on His example so I can know and follow it, and I have to abide in Him and open my heart to the blessed workings of His life in me.

5

As surely as Jesus conquered sin and its curse for me, He will conquer it and its power in me. What He began by His death for me, He will perfect by His life in me.

6

Taking up the cross and following Jesus is nothing less than living every day with our own lives and wills given up to death. The crucified Christ and the crucified Christian belong to each other. The Christian glories in the Cross because it makes him a partner in a death and victory that has already been accomplished and in which the deliverance from the powers of the flesh and of the world has been secured to him.

The Lord Jesus has shown us that the best place to practice self-denial is in our ordinary dealings with men.

7

How often we have asked to abide continually in Christ. We have thought of more study of the Word, more faith, and more prayer. We have overlooked the simple truth, *"If ye keep my commandments, ye shall abide in my love"* (John 15:10).

Giving up our wills to God is always the measure of His giving His power in us. A surrender to full obedience is nothing but a full faith that God will work all in us.

8

Who can say whether this is not one of the secrets that eternity will reveal, that sin was permitted because otherwise God's love could never have been so fully revealed? The highest glory of God's love was manifest in the self-sacrifice of Christ. Without entire self-sacrifice, we cannot love as Jesus loved.

9

It is only when we sacrifice ourselves to God that there will be the power for an entire self-sacrifice. When faith has first taken hold of the promise, *"Inasmuch as ye have done it unto one of the least of these my brethren, ye have done it unto me"* (Matt. 25:40), I will be able to understand the glorious harmony between sacrifice to God and sacrifice for men.

10

The freer the church is of the spirit and principles of the world, the more influence she will exert in it. The believer sees that the only way to answer his calling is by being crucified to the world. The only way to withdraw himself from its power is to live in Christ and to rely on Him to go into it and bless it. He lives in heaven and walks on earth.

11

The church of Christ in her mission, *"Go ye therefore, and teach all nations"* (Matt. 28:19), has the promise, *"Lo, I am with you alway"* (v. 20). The Lord does not demand anything that He does not give the power to perform. The Lord Jesus will give His people all the preparation they need.

12

Christ's mission is the only reason for our being on earth. Just as with Jesus, our heavenly mission demands nothing less than entire consecration.

The stronger the Christian's faith is in God's everlasting purpose, the more his courage for work will be strengthened. The more he works and is blessed, the clearer it will become that all is of God.

13

Sin had made us believe that it is a humiliation always to be seeking God's will. We did not know that the beauty, the unspotted purity of the robe of creature-hood, was its obedience. Christ put on that robe to show us how to wear it and how to enter into the presence and glory of God with it.

14

The great purpose of redemption was to make us and our will free from the power of sin and to lead us again to live and do the will of God. In His life on earth, Christ showed us what it is to live only for the will of God. In His death and resurrection, He won for us the power to live and do the will of God as He had done.

15

Sin is not in this: that man has a creature-will different from the Creator's. But, sin is in this: that man clings to his own will when it is seen to be contrary to the will of the Creator. Take God's will as one great whole, as the only thing for which you live on earth.

16

God's will only seems difficult when we look at it from a distance and are unwilling to submit to it. How beautiful the will of God makes everything in nature! The will of God is the will of His love. How can you fear to surrender yourself to it?

17

A hearty obedience to the commandments and a ready obedience to the conscience are the preparation that will lead you deeper into the application of the Word and into a more direct and spiritual insight into God's will with regard to yourself. It is to those who obey Him that God gives the Holy Spirit. And it is through the Holy Spirit that the blessed will of God becomes the light that shines ever more brightly on our path! *"If any man will do his will, he shall know"* (John 7:17).

18

A Christlike sense of Sonship will lead to a Christlike obedience.

The purpose of Christ's obedience was threefold: as our Example, to show us what true obedience is; as our Surety, by His obedience to fulfill all righteousness for us; and as our Head, to prepare a new and obedient nature to impart to us.

19

It was the compassionate sympathy of Jesus that attracted so many to Him on earth. More than anything, that same compassionate tenderness will still draw souls to you and your Lord.

20

In the Sermon on the Mount, Christ began with obedience. No one could enter the kingdom *"but he that doeth the will of my Father"* (Matt. 7:21). In the farewell discourse in the book of John, no words could express more simply or more powerfully the glorious place Christ gives to obedience. This obedience has a twofold possibility: it is only possible to a loving heart, and it makes possible all that God has to give of His Holy Spirit, of His wonderful love, and of His indwelling in Christ Jesus. I know of no Scripture that gives a higher revelation of the spiritual life, or the power of loving obedience as its one condition.

21

The desire for independence was the temptation in Paradise, and it is the temptation in each human heart. It seems hard to be nothing, to know nothing, and to will nothing. And yet it is so blessed. This dependence brings us into a most blessed communion with God. It takes from us all care and responsibility. It gives us real power and strength of will because we know that He works in us *"to will and to do"* (Phil. 2:13). It gives us the blessed assurance that our work will succeed because we have allowed God alone to take charge of it.

22

Although Jesus' life was strong and true, it could not bear the loss of direct and constant communion with the Father, with whom and in whom it had its being and its blessedness. Even work in the service of God and of love is exhausting. We cannot bless others without power going out from us. This must be renewed from above. It is from heaven alone that the power to lead a heavenly life on earth can come.

23

The entire sacrifice of ourselves to God in every prayer of daily life is the only preparation for those single hours of soul struggle in which we may be called to some special act of the surrender of the will that costs us tears and anguish. But he who has learned the former will surely receive strength for the latter.

24

When we behold the glory of God in Christ, in the mirror of the Holy Scriptures, His glory shines upon us and into us. This glory fills us until it shines out from us again. Beholding Jesus makes us like Him.

25

It is grace we need, not sin, to make and keep us humble. The most heavily laden branches always bow the lowest. The nearer the soul comes to God, the more His majestic presence makes it feel its smallness.

26

If the believer holds fast to what his participation with Christ's death signifies, he has the power to overcome sin. He cannot say, "Sin is dead," but the believer himself is dead to sin and alive to God. So then sin cannot for a single moment, without his consent, have dominion over him. If he sins, it is because he allows it to reign, and he submits himself to it.

27

Many have been looking most earnestly for full insight into the blessedness of being *"dead indeed unto sin, but alive unto God"* (Rom. 6:11) and yet have failed. They have been more occupied with the blessings to be had in Jesus, or with the effort to exercise a strong abiding faith in these blessings as theirs, than with Jesus Himself. And it is in Jesus that both the blessings and the faith that sees the blessings are ours.

28

It is as you bear the image of God here, as you live in the likeness of Jesus, who is the brightness of His glory and the express image of His person, that you will be fitted for the glory to come. If we are to bear the image of the heavenly, the Christ in glory, we must first bear the image of the earthly, the Christ in humiliation.

29

To be filled with the Holy Spirit, we must wait on our Lord in faith. His love desires to give us more than we know. You are in the Spirit as your vital air; the Spirit is in you as your life-breath. It is impossible to say what the Lord Jesus would do for a soul who is truly willing to live as entirely through Him as He lives through the Father.

30

With what care the tenderly sensitive film of the photographer is prepared to receive the impression. With what precaution its relative position to the object to be portrayed is adjusted. How still and undisturbed it is then held face to face with that object. Having done this, the photographer leaves the light to do its wonderful work, and his work is a work of faith. As the photographer believes in the power of the light to transcribe an image onto film, let us believe in the power of the light of God to transcribe Christ's image on our hearts. Let us not seek to do the work the Spirit must do. Let us simply trust Him to do it. Our duty is to seek the prepared heart: waiting, longing, and praying for the likeness. Our duty is to take our place face to face with Jesus: gazing, loving, believing that the wonderful vision of that Crucified One is the sure promise of what we can be. Then we can put aside all that can distract, and in stillness of soul, silent unto God, we can just allow the blessed Spirit, as the light of God, to do the work.

31

Before He gave His command and pointed to the great field of the world, Christ first drew the eyes of His servants to Himself on the throne. *"All power is given unto me in heaven and in earth"* (Matt. 28:18). Then followed, *"Lo, I am with you alway"* (v. 20). Between these two pillar promises of Christ's power in heaven and His presence on earth lies the gate through which the church enters to the conquest of the world.

April

April

1

Paul wrote, *"I lie not, my conscience also bearing me witness in the Holy Ghost"* (Rom. 9:1). The Holy Spirit speaks through conscience. He is the Voice of God.

Let your prayer closet be the classroom and your morning watch the study hour in which your relationship of entire dependence on and submission to the Holy Spirit's teaching is proved.

2

Love every believer not for the sake of what in him is in sympathy with you or pleasing to you, but for the sake of the Spirit of the Father that is in him.

3

The more the Spirit indwells you, and the mightier His working is, the more truly spiritual your being becomes. Self will sink away more, and the Spirit of Christ will use you more in building up and building together believers into a habitation of God.

4

The trust in gifts and knowledge, in soundness of creed and earnestness of work; the satisfaction in rituals and customs, leaves the flesh in full vigor, not crucified with Christ. So the Spirit is not free to work out true holiness in the Christian or a life in the power of Christ's love.

To be a Christian just means to have the Spirit of Christ, to have His love and to have been made by Him a fountain of love, springing up and flowing out in streams of living water.

5

Doing God's will is the only key to the knowledge of God's truth. Obedience on earth is the key to a place in God's love in heaven.

There is a general will of God for all His children, which we can, in some measure, learn from the Bible. But there is a special, individual application of the commands contained in the Bible, and this is God's will concerning each of us personally, which only the Holy Spirit can teach.

6

It is only where the soul gives the Spirit the precedence it claims, and self is denied to make way for God, that selfishness will be conquered and love toward our brothers will flow from love toward God.

7

Only the measure of real dependence on the Holy Spirit will decide the blessing and the power that it brings. The amount or the clearness or the interest of the Bible knowledge received will not bring such a blessing.

8

It is not the power of intellect, it is not even the earnest desire to know the truth, that fits a man for the Spirit's teaching. It is a life yielded to Him in waiting dependence and full obedience to be made spiritual that receives the spiritual wisdom and understanding.

9

Believe! It is not enough that the light of Christ shines on you in the Word. The light of the Spirit must shine in you.

10

It is the very work of the Spirit to unite Himself specially with what is material, to lift it up into His own Spirit nature, and so to develop what will be the highest type of perfection—a spiritual body.

11

In the Father, we have the unseen God, the Author of all. In the Son, we have God revealed and brought close. In the Spirit of God, we have the Indwelling God, the power of God dwelling in a human body and working in it what the Father and the Son have for us.

12

As all of the Word of God is given by the Spirit of God, so each word must be interpreted to us by that same Spirit. Not in the Spirit without the Word or with only a little of the Word, not in the Word without the Spirit or with only a little of the Spirit, but in the Word and Spirit is our assurance of safety in the path of the Spirit's guidance. Both must dwell richly within us, and both must be yielded to in implicit obedience.

13

The Holy Spirit is the church's power for all her work and her missions, and that power will only act mightily as the number of individual believers increases—believers who give themselves to be possessed, to be led, to be used by the Spirit of Christ.

14

When the Holy Spirit convinces us of the sin of the world, His work bears two marks. The one is the sacrifice of self, in the jealousy for God and His honor, combined with the deep and tender grief for the guilty. The other is a deep, strong faith in the possibility and power of deliverance.

15

God looks on the world in His holiness, hating its sin with such an infinite hatred and loving it with such a love that He gives His Son. The Son gave His life to destroy sin and to set its captives free.

Not in what we *know*, but in what we *are*, does the Spirit begin His work. And the teaching of the Spirit begins not in word or thought, but in power (1 Cor. 4:20).

16

There is no way of knowing the light but by being in it and using it. There is no way of knowing the Holy Spirit but by possessing Him and being possessed by Him. To have Him in us, doing His work and giving us His fellowship, is the path the Master opens when He says, *"Ye know him; for he...shall be in you"* (John 14:17).

17

However little we see or feel, let us believe. What is divine is always first known by believing. As we continue believing, we will be prepared to know and to see.

Gather together all that the Word says of the Spirit, His indwelling, and His work, and hide it in your heart. Be determined to accept nothing but what the Word teaches, but also to accept heartily all that it teaches.

18

God is to be found nowhere but in His will. His will in Christ, accepted and done by us with the heart, is the home of the Holy Spirit. Even now, day by day, we are to live in His glory. The Holy Spirit is able to be to us just as much as we are willing to have of Him and of the life of the glorified Lord.

19

Let us come under the hand of our Lord, covered by His hand with only one purpose: to have all our work covered in the hand of our God. There is the secret of life.

The Holy Spirit never looked for His own glory, never spoke of His own. His only purpose is to give glory to Christ. This decrease was not obligation but the yearning of His heart.

20

Learn to look on Jesus, and more and more you will find that Jesus, by His look, is taking your wandering look under the direction of the Holy Spirit. By and by it will become the very attitude of your soul, and you could do anything more easily than distrust Jesus.

Behind the valley of death there is an abundance of life, and the moment you give up all things, letting yourself go in the arms of Jesus, death will lose its terror.

21

The first great work of God with man was to get him to believe. All the dealings with individuals and with Israel had just this one purpose. Where He found faith, He could do anything. Unbelief was the root of disobedience and every sin. It made it impossible for God to do His work. The one thing God sought to awaken in men, by promise and threatening, by mercy and judgment, was faith.

22

A seed contains life hidden in the most dead, unlikely looking form possible, and this seed, with its hidden life, must itself again be hidden under the earth. So the kingdom of heaven comes to us in the seed of the Word. It must be hidden, not in the thoughts that we can recognize and watch over, but deeper down in the mysterious depths of the Spirit. Christ, who is in the unseen Spirit life of the Father, finds the unseen depths of our spirit life and enters there. He is Himself the Living Word, the Living Seed, the Spirit that is the life of the seed.

23

It is often only as we suffer in the flesh that the enlivening power of the Spirit is experienced. If one is to be led, one must follow; therefore, it is easily understood that to enjoy the leading of the Spirit, one must have a very teachable, following mind.

Even as beautiful flames on earth are nothing but the wood or coal transformed by the fire into its own light nature, so the fire of God cleanses and beautifies by filling the heart with its own heavenly glory.

In all our life processes, we must be made like Jesus. He received His life from God, and He lived it in dependence on God. He gave up His life to God, and He was raised from the dead by God. He lives His life in glory with God.

24

What a blessed solution God gives to all of our questions and our difficulties when He says, "My child, Christ has gone through it all for you!" He has worked out a new nature that can trust God, and Christ, the Living One in heaven, will live in you and enable you to live that life of trust.

25

Just as much as Christ was my substitute who died for me, He is as much my Head in whom and with whom I die. Just as He lives to intercede for me (Heb. 7:25), He lives to carry out and perfect His life in me. By His death, He proved that He possessed life only to hold it and to spend it for God.

26

Ask God to make you willing to believe with your heart that to die with Christ is the only way to live in Him. Jesus lived every day in the prospect of the Cross, and we, in the power of His victorious life, being made conformable to His death, must rejoice every day in going down with Him into death.

27

The acorn died, and the tree appeared. In the very grave where the acorn died, it stood there stretching its roots deeper and deeper into the earth yet growing higher, stronger, broader, and more beautiful. It owes all its fruit and all its foliage to that grave in which its roots are cast and kept. In the same way, Christ owes everything to His grave, and we, too, owe everything to the grave of Jesus.

28

Christ lost nothing by giving up His life unto the Father. If you want the glory and the life of God to come upon you, it is in the grave of utter helplessness that that life of glory will be born.

The secret of being inferior in nothing to even the chiefest apostles is this, as Paul said: *"I am nothing"* (1 Cor. 13:2). Why? Because *"God hath chosen the...things which are not"* (1 Cor. 1:27–28). Why? *"That no flesh should glory in his presence....He that glorieth, let him glory in the Lord"* (1 Cor. 1:29, 31). To be nothing is the only way to let God be all.

29

Jesus came to deliver man from sin and sickness so that He might make known the love of the Father.

In His actions, in the teaching of the disciples, in the work of the Holy Spirit, and in the words of the apostles, pardon and healing are always to be found together. To receive healing, it is necessary to begin by confessing sin and resolving to live a holy life. This is why those who receive healing receive a new spiritual blessing at the same time, feel more closely united to the Lord Jesus, and learn to love and serve Him better. The redeemed may always cry, *"Bless the LORD, O my soul...who forgiveth all thine iniquities; who healeth all thy diseases"* (Ps. 103:2–3).

30

The preaching of the Gospel and the healing of the sick are given as evident proof of Christ's mission as the Messiah (Matt. 11:5). Jesus, who took upon Him the soul and body of man, delivers both in equal measure from the consequences of sin. When Christ speaks of sickness, He always speaks of it as an evil caused by sin and Satan. He declared that every disciple would have to bear his cross (Matt. 16:24), but He never taught one sick person to resign himself to being sick. Sin in the soul and sickness in the body both bear witness to the power of Satan, and *"the Son of God was manifested, that he might destroy the works of the devil"* (1 John 3:8). Take a look at the following verses, which are examples of this: Job 2:7, Luke 13:16, Acts 10:38, Hebrews 2:14, and Genesis 1:31.

May

May

1

In our blessed Priest-King, Jesus Christ, the kingly power is founded on the priestly: *"He is able also to save...to the uttermost...seeing he ever liveth to make intercession"* (Heb. 7:25). In us, His priests and kings, it can be no other way.

As long as we look on prayer chiefly as the means of maintaining our own Christian life, we will not know fully what it is meant to be.

Jesus never taught His disciples how to preach, only how to pray. To know how to speak to God is more than knowing how to speak to man. Power with God is the first thing, not power with men. Do not be thinking of how little you have to bring God, but of how much He wants to give you.

2

The blessing does not depend on the strong or fervent feeling with which I pray, but on the love and the power of the Father to whom I entrust my needs. The knowledge of God's Father-love is the first and simplest, but also the last and highest, lesson in the school of prayer. The sooner I learn to forget myself in the desire that He may be glorified, the richer the blessing will be that prayer will bring to me. No one ever loses by sacrificing for the Father.

3

Because the will of God is the glory of heaven, doing His will is the blessedness of heaven. As His will is done, the kingdom of heaven comes into the heart and wherever faith has accepted the Father's will. The surrender to and the prayer for a life of heavenlike obedience is the spirit of childlike prayer.

As a child has to have an answer to a sum in order to show that he has done it correctly, so the proof that we have prayed rightly is the answer. In prayer and its answer, the interchange of love between the Father and His child takes place. Man's prayer on earth and God's answer in heaven are meant for each other. A life marked by daily answer to prayer is the proof of our spiritual maturity.

4

If the child is to know and understand his father; if as he grows up, he is to enter into all his will and plans; if he is to have his highest joy in the father, and the father in him, he must be of one mind and spirit with him. And so it is impossible to conceive of God bestowing any higher gift on His child than this, His own Spirit. God is what He is through His Spirit; the Spirit is the very life of God.

It is when we give ourselves to be a blessing that we can especially count on the blessings of God. The righteous man who is the friend of the poor is very specially the friend of God. This gives wonderful liberty in prayer. Every believer is a laborer. Every one of God's children has been redeemed for service and has his work waiting.

5

As long as we just pour out our hearts in a multitude of petitions while in prayer, without taking time to see whether every petition is sent with the purpose and expectation of getting an answer, not many will reach the mark. It is when in distinct matters we have in faith claimed and received answers that our more general prayers will be believing and effectual.

As we think of all He is and has, how He Himself is our life, we feel assured that we have only to ask and He will be delighted to take us up into closer fellowship with Himself and teach us to pray even as He prays. A life in God's infinite fatherliness and continual answers to prayer are inseparable, but the child who wants to know the love of the Father only when he has something to ask will be disappointed.

Faith is nothing except the purpose of the will resting on God's word and saying, "I must have it." To believe truly is to will firmly.

6

While praying, believe that you have now received the thing you asked for. It may only be later that you will see what you believe, but now without seeing, you are to believe that it has been given to you by the Father in heaven.

Faith says most confidently, "I have received the promise." Patience perseveres in prayer until the gift bestowed in heaven is seen on earth. Believe that you have received, and you will have! Between the "have received in heaven," and the "will have on earth," believe. Praise and prayer are linked through believing.

7

Let faith look to God more than to the thing promised. The cure of a feeble faith is to be found alone in the invigoration of our whole spiritual life by dealings with God. Learn to believe in God, to take hold of God, to let God take possession of your life, and it will be easy to take hold of the promise. He who knows and trusts God finds it easy to trust the promise, too.

8

Men of strong faith are men of much prayer. Much prayer, in closer union to Jesus, implies that the spirit of faith will come in power through the dying to self. Faith needs prayer for its full growth. It is only in a life of temperance and self-denial that there will be the heart or the strength to pray much. Without voluntary separation even from what is lawful, no one will attain any power in prayer.

9

My prayers are dealt with by God according to what I am when not praying, not what I try to be when praying.

Nothing would be more unnatural than that the children of a family should always meet their father separately and never in the united expression of their desires or their love. It is the union and fellowship of believers in which the Spirit can manifest His full power.

10

Man, in his spiritual nature, is under the law of gradual growth that reigns in all created life. It is only in the path of development that he can reach his divine destiny. The Father alone knows the moment when the soul or the church is ripened to that fullness of faith in which it can really take and keep the blessing. As a father, who longs to have his only child home from school and yet waits patiently until the time of training is completed, so it is with God and His children. He is the Long-suffering One and answers speedily.

11

Prayer teaches and gives strength for work, and work teaches and gives strength to pray. Faith is obedience at home and looking to the Master. Obedience is faith going out to do His will.

As a Christian grows in grace and in knowledge of the Lord Jesus, he is often surprised to find how the words of God grow, too, in the new and deeper meaning with which they come to him.

Just as far as we listen to the voice and language in which God speaks, and receive into our hearts God's thoughts, mind, and life through His words, we will learn to speak in the voice and language that God hears.

12

The Old Testament saints spoke in prayer. If the word was a command, they simply did as the Lord had spoken. Their lives were fellowship with God, the interchange of word and thought. What God spoke, they heard and did. What they spoke, God heard and did.

Let us believe that we can know if our prayers are according to God's will. Let us yield our hearts to have the Word of the Father dwell richly there. Let us live day by day with the anointing that teaches all things. Soon, we will understand how the Father's love longs that the child should know His will and should, in the confidence that His will includes all that His power and love have promised to do, know also that He hears the petitions that we ask of Him.

13

God wills a great deal of blessing to His people that never comes to them. He wills it most earnestly, but they do not will it. Thus, it cannot come to them.

Our true aim must not be to work much but to pray much and then to work enough for the power and blessing obtained in prayer to find its way through us to men.

Because we do not abide in Christ as He would have us to do, the church is ineffective in the presence of unbelief and worldliness and heathendom, in the midst of which the Lord is able to make her more than conqueror. Let us believe that He means what He promises, and let us accept the condemnation the confession implies.

14

The measure of believing, continued prayer will be the measure of the Spirit's working in the church. Direct, definite, determined prayer is what we need. The measure of God's giving the Spirit is the measure of our asking. He gives as a father to him who asks as a child.

There is nothing in honest business, when kept in its place as entirely subordinate to the kingdom, which must always be first, that need prevent fellowship with God.

15

A much-praying minister will receive entrance into God's will, of which he would otherwise know nothing; will be brought to praying people where he does not expect them; will receive blessing above all he asks or thinks. It is prayer that is the only secret of true church growth. Prayer is guided from heaven to find and send forth God-called and God-empowered men.

The attempt to pray constantly for ourselves must be a failure. Faith and love and perseverance will only be kindled in intercession for others. The power of the Spirit, which can fit us for saving men, also can only be found in intercession.

16

Intercession is the most perfect form of prayer. It is the prayer that Christ always prays on His throne. As love of our professions and Christian works and as delight in thoroughness and diligence sink away in the tender compassion of Christ, love will compel us to prayer because we cannot rest in our work if souls are not saved. True love must pray.

Just as the heaven that our natural eyes can see is one great ocean of sunshine with its light and heat-giving beauty and fruitfulness to earth, so Scripture shows us God's true heaven, filled with all spiritual blessings, divine light and love and life, heavenly joy and peace and power, all shining down upon us.

17

If we will only believe in God and His faithfulness, intercession will become to us the very first thing we take refuge in when we seek some blessing for others and the very last thing for which we cannot find time.

Prayer opens the way for God Himself to do His work in us and through us. As God's messengers, let our chief work be intercession. In it we secure the presence and power of God to go with us.

Let us confess before God our lack of prayer. Let us admit that the lack of faith, of which it is the proof, is the symptom of a life that is not spiritual, that is yet all too much under the power of self and the flesh and the world.

18

In all ages men have prayed under a sense that there were difficulties in the heavenly world to overcome. As they pleaded with God with the faith that could take hold of Him, and in that persevering supplication were brought into union with His will, the hinderances in themselves and in heaven were overcome together. As God conquered them, they conquered God. As God prevails over us, we prevail with God.

Faith in a prayer-hearing God will make a prayer-loving Christian. Where our life is right, we will know how to pray in order to please God, and prayer will secure the answer.

The man who is ready to risk all for God, can count on God to do all for him. It is as men live that they pray. It is life that prays.

19

The more we pray and the more conscious we become of our unfitness to pray in power, the more we will be urged and helped to press on toward the secret of power in prayer: a life abiding in Christ, entirely at His disposal.

The following sets apart the wholehearted believer from those of the world and worldly Christians around him: he lives consciously hidden in the secret of God's presence.

When the pressure of work for Christ is allowed to be the excuse for our not finding time to seek and secure His own presence and power in it, as our chief need, it most certainly proves that there is no right sense of our absolute dependence on God. There is then no true entrance into the heavenly, otherworldly character of our skills and aims, no full surrender to and delight in Jesus Christ Himself.

20

When once we see how there is to be nothing of our own for a single moment and that it is to be all Christ, moment by moment; once we learn to accept it from Him and trust Him for it, the life of Christ becomes the health of our soul. Health is nothing but life in its normal, undisturbed action. As Christ gives us health by giving us Himself as our life, so He becomes our strength for our walk. They who wait on the Lord will walk and not faint (Isa. 40:31), because Christ is now the strength of their lives.

21

The more heartily we enter into the mind of our blessed Lord and set ourselves simply just to think about prayer as He thought, the more surely will His words be like living seeds. They will grow and produce in us their fruit: a life and practice exactly corresponding to the divine truth they contain.

A Christian may often have very earnest desires for spiritual blessings. But alongside these there are other desires in his daily life occupying a large place in his interests and affections. The spiritual desires are not all-absorbing. He wonders why his prayer is not heard. It is simply that God wants the whole heart. *"The LORD our God is one LORD: and thou shalt love the LORD thy God with all thine heart"* (Deut. 6:4–5).

22

Prayer is just the breathing of the Spirit in us. Power in prayer comes from the power of the Spirit in us, waited on and trusted in. Failure in prayer comes from feebleness of the Spirit's work in us. To pray correctly, the life of the Spirit must be right in us.

As long as we measure our power for praying correctly and perseveringly, by what we feel or think we can accomplish, we will be discouraged when we hear of how much we ought to pray. But when we quietly believe that, in the midst of all our conscious weakness, the Holy Spirit, as a Spirit of Supplication, is dwelling within us for the very purpose of enabling us to pray in such manner and measure as God would have us, our hearts will be filled with hope.

23

The Spirit can pray in no other way in us than as He lives in us. It is only as we give ourselves to the Spirit living and praying in us that the glory of the prayer-hearing God, and the ever blessed and most effectual mediation of the Son, can be known by us in their power. When we realize how much time Christ spent in prayer and how the great events of His life were all connected with special prayer, we learn the necessity of absolute dependence on, and unceasing direct communication with, the heavenly world, if we are to live a heavenly life or to exercise heavenly power around us.

24

If anyone could have been satisfied with always living and working in the Spirit of prayer, it would have been our Master. But He could not. He needed to have His supplies replenished by continual and long-continued seasons of prayer. Christ was what

He taught. All His teaching was just the revelation of how He lived, and—praise God—of the life He was to lead in us.

Even as Christ obtained His right of prevailing intercession by His giving Himself as a sacrifice to God for men, and through it receives the blessings He dispenses, so we share His right of intercession if we have truly with Christ given ourselves to God for men. Then, we are able to obtain the powers of the heavenly world for them, too.

25

Tell everyone who is master of his own time that he is as the angels, free to tarry before the throne and then to go out and minister to the heirs of salvation.

We are frequently in danger of looking to what God has done and is doing and to count on that as the pledge that He will at once do more. And all the time it may be true that He is blessing us up to the measure of our faith or self-sacrifice, but then He cannot give a larger measure until there has been a new discovery and confession of what is hindering Him from giving a new blessing.

26

Men would gladly have a revival as the outgrowth of their agencies and progress. God's way is the opposite. It is out of death, acknowledged as the wages of sin, confessed as utter helplessness, that He revives. He revives the heart of the contrite one.

When earnest, godly workers allow, against their better judgment, the spiritual to be crowded out by incessant labor and the fatigue it brings, it must be because the spiritual life is not sufficiently strong in them. They need to put aside such occupations until the presence of God in Christ and the power of the Spirit have been fully secured.

27

It was when the friend at midnight, in answer to his prayer, had received from Another as much as he needed, that he could supply his hungry friend. It was the intercession, going out and importuning, that was the difficult work. Returning home with his rich supply to impart was easy, joyful work. This is Christ's divine order for all your work, my fellow believer: First come in utter poverty, every day, and get from God the blessing in intercession; go then, rejoicingly, to impart it.

28

On His resurrection day, our Lord gave His disciples the Holy Spirit to enable them to wait for the full outpouring on the Day of Pentecost. It is only in the power of the Spirit already in us, acknowledged and yielded to, that we can pray for His fuller manifestation. Say to the Father that it is the Spirit of His Son in you that is urging you to plead His promise.

Prayer is not only wishing or asking, but also believing and accepting.

29

In the last night, Christ asked three things for His disciples: that they might be kept as those who are not of the world, that they might be sanctified, and that they might be one in love. You cannot do better than to pray as Jesus prayed. Ask that God's people may be kept separate from the world and its spirit, that they, by the Holy Spirit, may live as those who are not of the world.

The utterances of our wishes give direction to the transactions in which we are engaged with God, and so awakens faith and expectation. Be very definite in your petitions, in order to know what answer you may look for.

30

The future of the church and the world depends, to an extent we little conceive, on the education of the day. The church may be seeking to evangelize the heathen while giving up her own children to secular and materialistic influences. Pray for schools and colleges, and that the church may realize and fulfill its momentous duty of caring for its children.

Beware in your prayer, above everything, of limiting God, not only by unbelief, but also by imagining that you know what He can do. Expect unexpected things, above all that we ask or think. Each time that you intercede, be quiet first and worship God in His glory.

Our great need is more of God.

31

Pray for the Jews. Their return to the God of their fathers stands connected, in a way we cannot tell, with wonderful blessing to the church and with the coming of our Lord Jesus.

All the powers of evil seek to hinder us in prayer. Prayer is a conflict with opposing forces. It needs the whole heart and all our strength. May God give us grace to strive in prayer until we prevail.

June

June

1

The benefit of discussing Scripture texts that are on a point or topic previously announced is very great. This practice leads to the searching of God's Word, as even preaching does not.

How many Bibles are being circulated? How many sermons on the Bible are being preached? How many Bibles are being read in home and school? How little blessing there is when it comes *"in word only";* and what divine blessing and power when it comes *"in the Holy Ghost"* (1 Thess. 1:5), when it is preached *"with the Holy Ghost sent down from heaven"* (1 Pet. 1:12).

2

Read a book to understand what is good, and then see if you receive benefit from the thoughts expressed. Read it to see if it is in accordance with God's Word. Read it to find out how your life corresponds with the good in it. See if your life has been in harmony with the new life. Direct your life for the future entirely according to God's Word.

3

One verse chosen to meet your needs that is read ten times and then laid up in your heart, is better than ten verses read once. Only as much of the Word as I actually receive and inwardly take hold of for myself is food for my soul.

As we see where, how often, and in what context a Bible word or a truth of the Christian life is found, its relative importance may be understood as well as its bearing on the whole of revelation.

4

With God, speaking and doing always go together. Will He say it and not do it? The deed follows the word. I hear what God has said. I take time to lodge in my heart the promised word, and I await the fulfillment. God promises, I believe, God fulfills. This is the secret of the new life.

5

The Christian only has to believe, and God will look to the fulfilling. One may think that he must have a great power to exercise such a great faith. You do not need to bring this mighty faith to get the Word fulfilled; the Word brings you this faith. The Word is living and powerful. Faith is by the Word. Keep yourselves occupied with the Word, and give it time. It will work in you a strong faith that can do anything.

6

If I trust in the Word and in the living God, His commandment will work in me the desire and power for obedience. When I weigh and hold fast to the command, it works the desire and the will to obey. It urges strongly the conviction that I can certainly do what my Father says. The Word, as the command of the living God who loves me, is my power.

If you study the Bible without an earnest and very definite purpose to obey, you are getting hardened in disobedience. You feel sure God gives the strength to do something only when you know that He is telling you to do it.

7

This is the love of God: not that He gives us something, but someone—a living person. He does not give us one or another blessing, but Him in whom all life and blessing exist—Jesus Himself. The whole of salvation consists in this: to have and to enjoy Jesus. *"He that hath the Son hath life"* (1 John 5:12).

8

God gives in a wonderful way. His methods are always the following: from the heart, completely for nothing, to the unworthy. And He gives completely. What He gives He will really make entirely our possession. To take Jesus, to hold Him fast, and to use Him when received, is our great work. And that taking is nothing but trusting. He is mine with all that He has.

9

In His great love, the Father gave the Son. Out of love, Jesus gave Himself. The taking, the having of Jesus, is the entrance to a life in the love of God. This is the highest life. Through faith we must press into love and dwell there.

10

Keep back no single sin. Keep back no single power. To save is to free from sin. Do not wait until you enter into temptation, but let your life beforehand always be through Jesus.

11

The continued vague confession of sin does more harm than good. It is much better to say to God that you have nothing to confess, because you have been prompt at confessing your sins as soon as you are aware that you have committed them, than to confess your general sinful nature out of a false sense of obligation to do so.

12

The secret of progress in the service of God is a strong yearning to become free from every sin and a hunger and thirst after righteousness. The Spirit of God is named the Holy Spirit because He makes us holy. Being right with God is followed by doing right.

13

You must love, although you do not feel the least love. It is not in your feeling, but in faith, that the Spirit in you will work in you all that the Father bids you. Therefore, although you feel absolutely no love for your enemy, say, "In faith in the hidden working of the Spirit in my heart, I do love him."

14

The nearer we are to God, the less we are in ourselves and the stronger we are in Him. The more I see of God, the less I become and the deeper my confidence in Him is. To become lowly, let God fill your sight and your heart. Where God is all, there is no time or place for man.

15

You often pray and strive against a sin. Although this is done with God's help, you want to be the person who would overcome. No! *"The battle is not yours, but God's"* (2 Chron. 20:15). Ask only: "What is my Jesus able to do?" What you really trust Him with, He is able to keep. You can trust the power of Jesus, if you know that He is yours if you converse with Him as your friend.

16

The following expression is altogether outside of the New Testament: "The Lord must help me to overcome sin." The grace of God in the soul does not become a help to us. He will do everything. When you surrender anything to the Lord for keeping, take heed that you give it wholly into His hands and that you leave it there. He will carry out your case gloriously.

17

The complaint about weakness is often nothing other than an apology for our idleness. There is power to be obtained in Christ for those who will take the pains to have it. Strength is for work. He who would be strong simply to be pious will not be so. He who in his weakness begins to work for the Lord will become strong.

18

Believing in opposition to what we see gives salvation. The unbelief that wants to see will not see.

The faith that does not yet see, but has enough in God, will see the glory of God. Feeling always seeks something in itself; faith keeps itself occupied with what Jesus is.

19

Our work every day and the whole day is to believe. All blessings and powers, as well as the victory for overcoming, come out of faith. The blessing of God includes in it the power of life for multiplication, for expansion, and for communication. In the Scriptures, blessing and multiplication go together. Blessing always includes the power to bless others.

20

Jesus left the throne of heaven for missions. The heathen are His inheritance. In heathendom, the power of Satan has been established, and Jesus must have Himself vindicated as the conqueror. The Lord has made Himself dependent on His body to do His work. It is the work for which the Holy Spirit was given. See this in the leading of the Spirit granted to Peter and Barnabas and Saul. Missionary work brings blessing on the church. It rouses Christians to heroic deeds of faith and self-denial. It has furnished the most glorious instances of the wondrous power of the Lord. In love for missionary work, you will learn to cleave to God and the Word; you will be drawn into prayer.

21

Gladness in God is the strongest proof that in God I have what satisfies me. Gladness is the token of the truth and the worth of obedience, showing I have pleasure in the will of God. The light of God's countenance gives the Christian his gladness. In fellowship with his Lord, the Christian will always be happy. The love of the Father shines like the sun upon His children. Sin makes dark; unbelief also makes dark, for it turns us from Him, who alone is the light.

22

Gladness is hindered by ignorance when we do not understand God and His love and the blessedness of His service. Gladness is also hindered by double-heartedness when we are not willing to give up everything for Jesus. Do not seek gladness. In that case you will not find it, because you are seeking feeling. But seek Jesus, follow Jesus, believe in Jesus, and gladness will be added to you.

23

Give yourself to Him, not to be saved from disobedience so that you may be happy now and live your own life without sinning and trouble. No, but give yourself to Him so that He may have you wholly for Himself as a surrendered vessel that He can fill with Himself, with His life and love for men.

24

The will of God is as perfect as He Himself is. Let us not be afraid to surrender ourselves to it. No one suffers loss by deeming the will of God unconditionally good.

The sure confidence of an answer is the secret of powerful praying. For a blessed prayer meeting, there must be love and unity among the suppliants, agreement on the definite object that is desired, the coming together in the name of Jesus, and the consciousness of His presence. The power of your prayer will be according to your conviction of the nearness of God.

25

When the Lord Jesus manifests His great grace to a soul in redeeming it, He desires that the world should see and know it. He wants to be known and honored as its proprietor. Apart from this public confession, surrender is only halfhearted.

26

Conformity to the world can be overcome by nothing but conformity to Jesus. Conformity to the world is strengthened especially by dealings with it. It is in dealings with Jesus that we will adopt His mode of thinking, His disposition, and His manners. This is the spirit of the world: to seek one's self and the visible. The Spirit of Jesus is this: to live for God and the things that are invisible.

27

Do not use the day of rest only as a day for the public observance of divine worship. In the church you have the ordinances of preaching and united prayer and praise to keep you occupied. But, it is especially in private personal communion that God can bless and sanctify you.

The holy day at the opening of the week is appointed, not that we might have at least one day of rest, but that it might fit us to carry God's holy presence into all the week and its work. *"If the firstfruits be holy, the lump is also holy: and if the root be holy, so are the branches"* (Rom. 11:16).

28
The lessons of Communion are many. It is a feast of remembrance, a feast of reconciliation, a covenant feast, and a feast of hope. But all these separate thoughts are only subordinate parts of the principal element, which is that the living Jesus would give Himself to us in the most inward union.

29
There is only one Hebrew word for both "obeying voice" and "hearing voice." When I learn the will of God, not in the words of a man or a book, but from God Himself, I will surely believe what is promised and do what is commanded. The Holy Spirit is the voice of God, and when we hear the living voice, obedience becomes easy.

30
Read the Word with a searching of the Scriptures. The best explanation of the Bible is the Bible itself. Take three or four texts on a point and compare them. See where they agree and where they differ, where they say the same thing or something else. Let the Word of God be cleared up and confirmed by what God said at another time on the same subject. The sacred writers used this method of instruction with the Scriptures.

July

July

1

The secret of the life of holiness comes to those who do not seek it, but only seek Jesus. Let us all learn to trust in Jesus and to rejoice in Him even though our experience is not what we would wish. He will make us holy. But whether we have entered the blessed life of faith in Jesus as our sanctification, or are still longing for it from afar, we all need one thing: the simple believing and obedient acceptance of each word that our God has spoken.

2

"Be ye holy; for I am holy" (1 Pet. 1:16). It is as if God said, "Holiness is My blessedness and My glory; without this you cannot see Me or enjoy Me. There is nothing higher to be conceived of. I invite you to share with Me in it; I invite you to become like Myself. *'Be ye holy; for I am holy.'*"

3

Holiness is not something we do or attain. It is the communication of the divine life, the inbreathing of the divine nature, and the power of the divine presence resting on us. The Holy One calls us to Himself so that He may make us holy in possessing

Him. It is because the call to holiness comes from the God of infinite power and love that we may have the confidence that we can be holy.

4

The nature of light is the same whether in the sun or in a candle. The nature of holiness remains unchanged whether it is God or man in whom it dwells. The more carefully we listen to God's voice and let it sink into our hearts, the more all human standards will fall away. Then only the following words will be heard: *"Holy; for I am holy"* (Lev. 11:44).

All God's teaching about holiness is comprised in three great lessons: first, a revelation, *"I am holy"* (Lev. 11:44); second, a command, *"Be ye holy"* (Lev. 20:7); third, a gift, the link between the two, "You are holy in Christ."

5

We are holy in Christ Jesus. If we would only believe, how God's light would shine and fill our hearts with joy and love. Let us fear our own thoughts and crucify our own wisdom. Let us give ourselves up to receive, in the power of the life of God Himself working in us by the Holy Spirit, that which is deeper and truer than human thought—Christ Himself as our holiness.

6

Since the revelation of the Holy One of old was a very slow and gradual one, let us be content to follow patiently, step by step, the path of the shining light through the Word. It will shine more and more unto the perfect day (Prov. 4:18).

7

Why have so many believers seen so little of the beauty of the new covenant life, with its power of holy and joyful obedience? The Lord was with the disciples, but *"their eyes were holden that they should not know him"* (Luke 24:16). It is with many as with Elisha's servant: all heaven is around them, and they do not know it. Nothing will help but the prayer, *"LORD...open* [their] *eyes, that* [they] *may see"* (2 Kings 6:17).

8

The consciousness of God's presence, making and keeping us His very own, works the true separateness of the world and its spirit from ourselves and our will. As this separation is prized and persevered in, the holiness of God will enter in and take possession.

9

Because God is a spiritual and invisible Being, every revelation of Himself, whether in His work, His Word, or His Son, calls for faith. Faith is to the soul what the senses are to the body. By it alone we enter into communication and contact with God. Faith is that meekness of soul that waits in stillness to hear, to understand, and to accept what God says; to receive, to retain, and to possess what God gives. By faith we allow God to become our very life. And because holiness is God's highest glory and blessing, it is especially in the life of holiness that we need to live by faith alone.

10

True holiness, God's holiness, works itself out in us in love, in seeking and loving the unholy so that they, too, may become holy. Self-sacrificing love is of the very essence of holiness.

11

The will of God must first live in us if it is to be done by us. The way for us to have God's power in us is for ourselves to be in His power. Put yourself into the power of God. Let the Holy Spirit dwell within as in His holy temple, revealing the Holy One on the throne, ruling all. Holiness is essential to effectual service.

12

If in our study of the way of holiness there has been awakened in us the desire to accept and adore and stand complete in all the will of God, let us seek to recognize that will in everything that comes on us. The sin of him who vexes us is not God's will. But it is God's will that we should be, in that position of difficulty, tried and tested. Such acceptance of the trial turns it into a blessing. It will lead on to an ever clearer abiding in all the will of God, all day.

13

The more deeply we enter by faith into our liberty that we have in Christ, the more joyfully and confidently we present our members to God as instruments of righteousness. The liberty is not lawlessness. We are delivered from our enemies so that we may serve Him in righteousness and holiness all the days of our lives.

14

The secret of true holiness is a very direct and personal relationship to the Holy One. All the teaching through the Word or men should be made entirely dependent on and subordinate to the personal teaching of the Holy Spirit.

15

How many weary workers there are mourning the lack of power. They have spent their strength more in the outer court of work and service than in the inner life of fellowship and faith.

16

It is wonderful to think that the everlasting God who created heaven and earth should deal with each one of us individually, and that it should please Him to fill us with that everlasting love in which the Father begot the Son and in which the Holy Spirit maintains the fellowship between Father and Son.

17

I must not seek for love, but for God, for love is the very nature of God. Scripture does not say, "God has love," but, *"God is love"* (1 John 4:8), and the love that I need is God Himself coming into my heart. When the soul is perfected in love, it has such a sense of that love that it can rest in it for eternity, and though it has as much as it can contain for the time being, it can always receive more.

18

If we loved others with the love of God, how much more power there would be in our work, how much more intercession, how much we would sacrifice everything, our formality, our habits. We would do work breathed upon by the love of God.

It is only the love of God coming in that will cast out self, but self must be brought as a criminal to His feet. When God brings a man to see all that there is in Christ and to receive Christ fully, the power of Christ's death can come upon him, and he can die to sin. If he dies to sin, he dies to self.

19

Christ appealed to the law. He had come to secure its fulfillment. He said to the young ruler, *"Thou knowest the commandments"* (Mark 10:19). He revealed the new law of love. An unforgiving spirit, unloving thoughts and sharp words, and the neglect to do good, are all so much disobedience. He spoke much of self-denial. Self is the root of all lack of love and obedience, the source of all sin. Christ's disciple must *"deny himself, and take up his cross"* (Matt. 16:24) and become the *"servant of all"* (Mark 9:35). Christ claimed for God the love of the whole heart.

20

The work of God the Father is to beget God the Son, and that is the work that goes on through eternity. God has nothing for us but Jesus, but He is willing to give this—the living Son, born afresh into us. When the living Christ dwells in us, He will break open the fountain of love within us.

21

Love means giving and giving all. God gave His Son to me, and with Him, He gave all. Now, love is God claiming everything. In the light of Christ's love, perfect love means that we give up ourselves to pray and to work for others.

The love and the faith of Christ's disciples were very defective, yet Christ accepted it as the obedience and the faith of loving hearts. So, if we come to Christ with our feeble beginnings, He will receive our love and will lead us day by day in the path of perfect love and perfect obedience.

Just as we must be separate from the world and joined to Christ in obedience to His Word, so we must also be joined to each other.

22

A child may be the perfect image of his father. There may be a great difference in power, and yet the resemblance may be so striking that everyone notices it. So a child of God, though infinitely less than the Father, may yet bear the image of the Father so markedly that in his human life, he will be perfect as the Father is in His divine life.

Man was created simply to show forth God's glory by allowing God to show how completely He could reveal His likeness and blessedness in man. A life that is lived wholly for God has been accepted by the Father in all ages as the mark of the perfect man.

23

The work of a child is very defective and yet the cause of joy and hope to a father, because he sees in it proof of the child's attachment and obedience, as well as the pledge of what that spirit will do for the child when his intelligence and his strength have been increased. The child has served the father with a perfect heart, though the perfect heart does not at once imply perfect work.

24

If we are to have perfect peace and confidence, we must know that our heart is perfect with God. The consciousness of a perfect heart gives wonderful power in prayer. It is only he who knows most of what it is to be perfect in purpose who will pray most to be perfect in practice, too. Walking before God will ensure walking in His commandments.

Faith expects from God what is beyond all expectation.

25

To have God reveal His strength in us, to have Him make us strong for life or work, for doing or for suffering, our hearts must be perfect with Him.

God is love. He does not live for Himself, but in the energy of an infinite life makes His creatures, as far as they can possibly receive it, partakers of His perfection. As little as there can be a ray of light, however dull and clouded it may be, unless it comes from the sun, so little can there be any perfection unless it comes from God.

26

A man may have his heart intent on serving God perfectly, and yet he may be unconscious of how very imperfect his knowledge of God's will is. The soul that longs to be perfect in its way, and in deep consciousness of its need of a divine teaching pleads for it, will not be disappointed.

27

"Let us go on unto perfection" (Heb. 6:1) means the following: let us go on to know Christ perfectly,

to live entirely by His heavenly life now that He is perfected, and to follow wholly His earthly life and the path in which He reached perfection.

There must be harmony between the place of worship and the worshippers. As He has prepared the perfect sanctuary, the Holiest of All, for us, so He has prepared us for it, too.

On our part, the surrender to be made perfect will be the measure of our capacity to understand what God has done in Christ.

28

A valuable piece of machinery may be out of order. The owner has spent time and trouble in vain to fix it. The maker comes, and it costs him only a moment to remove the hindrance. In the same way, the soul that has wearied itself for years in the effort to do God's will may often in one moment be delivered from some misunderstanding as to what God demands or promises. Then, it will find itself restored and perfected for every good thing. What was done in a moment becomes the secret of the continuous life, as faith each day claims the God who perfects, to do that which is well pleasing in His sight.

29

Jesus Christ was Himself not perfected in one day. In Him patience had its perfect work. True faith recognizes the need for time, and it rests in God. The weakest point in the character of the Christian is the measure of His nearness to perfection. It is in the little things of daily life that perfection is attained and proved.

30

There is the inward perfection that comes from growth and development, and the perfection that consists in having defects removed and what is lacking supplied. Only the former could be used of the Lord Jesus, not the latter. Both have reference to what God seeks in His children and works in them.

No one will pray for the perfected heart earnestly, perseveringly, believingly, until he accepts God's Word fully that it is a positive command and an immediate duty to be perfect.

31

The consciousness of the utter impossibility of attempting obedience in human strength will soon grow strong. The faith that the word of command was simply meant to draw the soul to Him who gives will also grow. The will of God is the expression of the divine perfection.

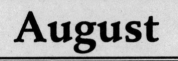

August

August

1

Peter wanted to walk like Christ so that he might get near Christ. He did not say: "Lord, let me walk around the sea here," but, "Let me come to You." When Peter was in the boat, what did he have between him and the sea? A couple of planks. But when he stepped out on the water, what did he have between him and the sea? Not a plank, but the word of the Almighty Jesus.

2

The Christian life can be compared to Peter walking on the waves: nothing is as difficult and impossible without Christ. Nothing is as blessed and safe with Christ. Peter walked back to the boat without sinking again. Christ took him by the hand and helped him. They were very near to each other, and it was the nearness to his Lord that strengthened him. It is possible to be far nearer to Christ after failure than before.

3

How often we worry about things, and about praying for them, instead of going back to the root of things and saying: "Lord, I only crave to be the receptacle of what the will of God means for me, of what the power and the gift and the love and the Spirit of God mean for me."

You can never have too strong a will. The trouble is that we do not give the strong will up to God to make it a vessel in which He can and will pour His Spirit, in order to fit it to do splendid service for Himself. Does God not give us all good gifts to enjoy? But the reality of the enjoyment is in the giving back.

4

Have I not seen a mother give a piece of cake to her child, and then the child offers her a piece? How the mother values the gift. Your God, the Father's heart of love, longs to have you give Him everything. He knows that every gift you bring will bind you closer to Himself, every surrender will open your heart wider to get more of His spiritual gifts.

When God's Word comes close to you and touches your heart, remember that it is Christ, out of whose mouth goes the two-edged sword. It is Christ in His love coming to cut away the sin so that He may fill your heart with the blessing of God's love.

5

Do not ask, "Can I be kept from sinning if I keep close to Him?" but ask, "Can I be kept from sinning if He always keeps close to me?" You will then see at once how safe it is to trust Him.

I may point men to Jesus as earnestly as I can, but it will avail little unless I lead them to believe that they must have the Holy Spirit in them to reveal Christ to them.

6

As our whole life becomes filled with the humbling, solemn, subduing presence of God through the Holy Spirit, we will walk about like men of God among people. We will not be men who vaguely preach about the Book and what is in the Book, but we will be those who preach what they are and what they have seen of Jesus.

7

When the Holy Spirit comes within us as the fire of God's love for souls, there will come to us an intensity and desire too deep for words. This is the time when the Holy Spirit prays in us with *"groanings which cannot be uttered"* (Rom. 8:26).

The following is a threefold cord that cannot be broken: love in the Spirit to each other and to all believers, prayer in the name of Jesus, and God to be waited on and trusted.

It is not always more work that is needed. Some might work less and yet do better work. The main thing is the quality of work that is done.

8

What was to bring conviction that Jesus was the Christ? Love. This is what Christ said: *"I pray...that they all may be one...that the world may know that thou hast sent me"* (John 17:15, 21, 23).

Not preaching, but love. Preaching is needed—praise God for what it does!—but love will do more.

9

The Son of God came to earth to prove that the love of God in heaven could stand the trial of life—every enmity, every shame, every suffering—and live through it all. It is your high privilege to have your heart filled with the heavenly love of Christ Jesus and to carry it through this life.

10

I feel more and more deeply that a Christian may be earnest and yet his or her life may be far below what God could make it if he or she would wait for the Holy Spirit to get possession.

We should continually, in our prayers and in our life, let this thought be our joy and our strength: however ignorant I feel, and however feeble my words have been, the Spirit prays in me, and God who searches hearts knows the mind of the Spirit.

The consciousness of ignorance lies at the root of true teachableness. *"The meek will he guide in...his way"* (Ps. 25:9). Head knowledge only gives human thoughts without power. God, by His Spirit, gives a living knowledge that enters the love of the heart, and works completely.

11

How does God teach His eaglet children to use their wings? He comes and stirs up their nests with some tribulation or temptation. Why? Just as the eaglets find the mother coming under them and carrying them as they are ready to sink, so the everlasting arms are stretched out underneath the soul that feels itself ready to perish. As the eaglet trusts the mother to carry it, so my God asks me to trust Him to bear me.

12

The everlasting God does not faint and is not weary. He gives power to the faint and to them who have no might. He increases strength (Isa. 40:28–29). If the everlasting God is never weary, you do not ever need to be weary, because your God is your strength. You have no strength but what God gives, and you can have all the strength that God can give.

Study and love your Bible. However, remember it is God who must give the orders, and you will fail if you take them from a book. Love your Bible, and fill your heart with it, but let God apply it in your daily life.

13

The great secret of a right waiting on God is to be brought down to utter inability: *"I do nothing of myself"* (John 8:28). Jesus said that, and He just waited on God. Would you not like to occupy the very place that Jesus did before the Father and in the Father's heart? Would you not be willing to take that place and to love every day as a man who has no might but is utterly helpless, and be willing just to wait on God?

14

We must not only think of our waiting on God, but also of what is more wonderful still: of God's waiting on us. If He waits for us, then we are more than welcome. Who can measure the difference between the great sun and a little blade of grass? Yet the grass has all of the sun it can need or hold. In waiting on God, His greatness and your littleness suit and meet each other most wonderfully.

15

Christ not only said, *"Abide in me,"* but also, *"I in you"* (John 15:4). The Epistles speak not only of us in Christ, but also of Christ in us, the highest mystery of redeeming love. As we maintain our place in Christ day by day, God waits to reveal Christ in us.

16

There is such a danger of our being so occupied with the things that are coming more than with Him who is to come. Nothing but humble waiting on God can save us from mistaking intellectual study for the true love of Him and His appearing. We are in the Lord's place, not when we are most occupied with prophetic subjects, but when in humility and love we are clinging close to our Lord and His followers.

17

Scripture was not written to increase our knowledge, but it was written so that the man of God may be perfect, thoroughly furnished for all good works (2 Tim. 3:16–17). *"If any man will do his will, he shall know"* (John 7:17). If a man's heart is given up to do God's will, as far as he knows it, he will know what God has to teach him further. It is simply what is true of every scholar with his studies, of every apprentice with his trade, of every man in business—doing is the one condition of confidently knowing.

18

The activity of the mind, in studying the Word or giving expression to its thoughts in prayer, may so engage us that we do not come to the still waiting on the All-glorious One.

In Scripture we have the words of daily life. They, of themselves, are without life or power. The mind can study and utter them, but they bring neither help nor blessing. *"The letter killeth, but the spirit giveth life"* (2 Cor. 3:6). The fire of the Holy Spirit takes them as its fuel and makes them the power by which the fire on the altars of our hearts is always kept burning.

19

If we seek above everything to be freed from our sins and to have the baptism of the Spirit, so that Christ and His will may have the complete mastery in us; if we seek it for the sake of God's holiness, so that He may be glorified and Christ be all, our happiness and our usefulness will come of themselves.

20

From the commencement of His public life to its close, Christ lived by the Word of God. *"It is written"* (Matt. 4:4) was the word with which He conquered Satan. *"The spirit of the Lord GOD is upon me"* (Isa. 61:1) was the consciousness with which He opened His preaching. *"That the scripture might be fulfilled"* (John 17:12) was the light in which He gave Himself to the death. After the Resurrection, He expounded *"in all the scriptures the things concerning himself"* (Luke 24:27).

21

It is a terrible mistake to think that when once a man is filled with the Spirit, persistent study of God's Word and reverent, wholehearted submission to it are not as much needed as before. *"The priest shall burn wood on* [the altar] *every morning"* (Lev. 6:12).

22

Often Christian liberty is spoken of as freedom from restraint in sacrificing our will or the freedom to enjoy the world. Its real meaning is the very opposite. True love asks to be free from self and the world to bring its all to God. The truly free spirit asks: "How far am I free to follow Christ to the uttermost?"

23

Give up yourself to God's perfect love to work out His perfect will. He will surely give you light and strength for all He means you to do. The throne of the Lamb is certainly proof that there is no sure way for us to have riches and honor other than through His poverty.

24

The soul that in simplicity yields to the leading of her Lord will find that the fellowship of His suffering brings the fellowship of His glory even here. *"Though he was rich, yet for your sakes he became poor, that ye through his poverty might be rich"* (2 Cor. 8:9).

25

This is the chief mark and glory of the Son of God: that He lived and died, not for Himself, but for others. It was to do God's will that Christ came from heaven. It is to do God's will in you that He has entered your heart. Jesus won back for us the life man had been created for, with God dwelling in him, by giving to us His life, the very life He had lived.

26

All the sin of heathendom, all the sin of Christendom, is but the outgrowth of the one root—God dethroned and self enthroned in the heart of man.

The mark of a kingdom is the presence of the king. Through the Holy Spirit, Christ came down to be with His disciples as truly and more nearly than when in the flesh. The disciples had their Lord with them as consciously as the angels in heaven have Him. His presence made heaven to be all around and in them.

27

Think of the work Christ's disciples, who were simple fishermen, dared to undertake and were able to accomplish, their weapon being the despised Gospel of the crucified Nazarene. See how the coming of the kingdom brought a new power from heaven by which feeble men were made mighty through God, and the slaves of Satan were made God's holy children.

28

In the feebleness of the grave Jesus gained His throne. We need to die with Him; that is the way to get delivered from self, the way to receive the heavenly life as a little child and so to enter the kingdom. The feebleness of Bethlehem and the manger, of Calvary and the grave, were Christ's way into the kingdom. For us there is no other way.

29

As we seek to humble ourselves and to renounce all wish and all hope of being, or doing, good of ourselves; as we yield all our human ability and energy to the death, in the confession that it is nothing but sinful and worthy of death, God's Spirit will make the power of Christ's death to sin work in us. We will die with Him, and with Him be raised in newness of life. The new life will be the little child who receives the kingdom.

30

How seldom we think that our hearts were actually created so that God might live there, that He might show forth His life and love there, and that our love and joy might be in Him alone. How little we know that just as naturally as we have the love of parents or of children filling our hearts and making us happy, we can have the living God, for whom the heart was made, dwelling there and filling it with His own blessedness and goodness.

31

Say to God, "Father, here am I for You to give as much of Christ's likeness in me as I can receive."

Then, wait to hear Him say, "My child, I give you as much of Christ as your heart is open to receive."

The manna of one day was spoiled when the next day came (Exod. 16:19–21). I must have fresh grace from heaven every day, and I can obtain it only in direct waiting on God Himself.

September

September

1

What is the difference between a dead Christ whom the women went to anoint and a living Christ? I must do everything for a dead Christ; a living Christ does everything for me.

An unseen, silent influence comes out from man in proportion as he has the very spirit and presence of Jesus upon him, not as a sentiment or an aspiration, but in reality. That secret influence is the holy presence of Jesus.

2

It is not your faith that will keep you standing, but it is a living Jesus, met every day in fellowship and worship and love. Ask Him, "Jesus, You have told me to believe, to obey, and to abide near You; is there anything more I need in order to secure the enjoyment of Your abiding presence?" And He will reply, "I have redeemed you to be a witness, to go out into the world confessing Me before men." Work for Him who is worthy. His blessing and His presence will be found in the work.

3

You often try hard to trust God, and you fail. Why? Because you have not taken time first to see

God. How can you trust God fully until you have met Him and known Him?

When God wanted to send any man upon His service, He first met him and talked with him and cheered him time after time. God appeared to Abraham seven or eight times and gave him one command after another, and so Abraham learned to obey Him perfectly. God appeared to Joshua and to Gideon, and they obeyed. Why are we not obedient? Because we have so little of this near fellowship with Jesus.

4

We read, *"The spirit of the LORD* [clothed] *Gideon"* (Judg. 6:34). In the New Testament there is an equally wonderful text: *"Put ye on the Lord Jesus Christ"* (Rom. 13:14), that is, clothe yourself with Christ Jesus. That does not only mean by inspiration of righteousness outside of me, but also to clothe myself with the living love of the living Christ. He whom I have to put on is like a garment covering my whole being.

5

There are many Christians who know that they must believe not only in a crucified Christ, but also in a living Christ. They try to grasp it, but it does not bring them a blessing. Why? Because they want to *feel* it and not to *believe* it. They want to work for it and with efforts get hold of it, instead of just quietly sinking down and believing, "Christ, the living Jesus, He will do everything for us."

Just as a living child lives day by day in the arms of its mother and grows up year by year under a mother's eye, it is a possibility that you can live every day and hour of your life in fellowship with the Holy Jesus.

6

The great thing in prayer is to feel that we are putting our supplications into the bosom of omnipotent Love. Before and above everything, let us take time before we pray to realize the glory and presence of God.

"God first" is a motto often misunderstood. God first may mean "I" second. God is thus first in order, but one of a series of powers. The meaning of the words is really, "God all, everything."

Christ cannot help coming in where there is a living faith, a full faith. Let us believe, because *"all things are possible to him that believeth"* (Mark 9:23). That is God's Word.

7

What is to make a difference between Christ's disciples and other people? It is this, to be in fellowship with Jesus every hour of the day. Christ is now able to do in heaven what He could not do when He was on earth—to keep in the closest fellowship with every believer throughout the whole world. Why was my Lord Jesus taken up to heaven away from the life of earth? Because the life of earth is confined to localities, but the life in heaven is a life in which there is no limit, no bound, no locality. Christ was taken up to heaven so that, in the power of the omnipresent God, He might be able to fill every individual here and be with every individual believer.

8

When we have Jesus with us, and when we go every footstep with the thought that it is Jesus who sends us and is helping us, then there will be brightness in our testimony. It will help other believers to say, "I see why I have failed. I took the word and the blessing as I thought I took the life, but I was without the living Jesus."

Just as truly as Christ was with Peter in the boat, just as Christ sat with John at the table, that is as truly as I can have Christ with me. I can have Him more actually, for they had their Christ in the body—He was a man, an individual separate from them—but I may have the glorified Christ in the power of the throne of God, the omnipotent, omnipresent Christ.

9

Why did God give the angels or man a self? God gave me the power of self-determination so that I might bring this self every day and say: "Oh, God, work in it; I offer it to You."

God's Word teaches us that God does not expect a man to live as he ought for one minute unless the Holy Spirit is in him to enable him to do it.

Did a father or mother ever think, "Today I want my child to love me"? No, they expect the love every day. So God wants His child every moment to have a heart filled with the love of the Spirit.

10

Suppose a painter had a piece of canvas on which he desired to work out some beautiful design.

If it does not belong to him, and anyone has a right to take it and to use it for any other purpose, do you think the painter would bestow much work on that? No. Yet people want Jesus Christ to bestow His effort upon them in taking away this temper or that other sin, though in their hearts they have not yielded themselves utterly to His command and His keeping. If you will come and give your whole life into His charge, Christ Jesus is mighty to save and waits to fill you with His Spirit.

11

Fellowship with the Cross of Christ will be an unceasing denial of self, every hour and every moment by the grace of God.

If I know that God is my God, not through man's teaching or with my mind or my imagination, but in the living evidence that God gives in my heart, then I know that the divine presence of my God will be so wonderful. My God Himself will be so beautiful, so near, that I can live all my days and years a conqueror through Him who loved me (Rom. 8:37).

12

A pointer helps to show a place on the map. The pointer might be of fine gold, but we want to see what it points at. The Bible is nothing but a pointer, pointing to God, and—may I say it with reverence—Jesus Christ came to point us, to show us the way. He died so that He might bring us to God.

When a tree of one hundred years old was first planted, God did not give it a stock of life by which to carry on its existence. Every year God clothes the tree with its foliage and its fruit, and that is what God is for: to work in us by His mighty operation without one moment's ceasing.

13

Has God arranged that the light of the sun, which will one day be burned up, can come to you unconsciously and shine on you blessedly and mightily? Is God not willing, or not able, to let His light and His presence shine through you so that you can walk all day with God nearer to you than anything in nature?

What is religion? Religion is just as much as you have of God working in you. If you want more religion, more strength, more fruitfulness, you must have more of God.

14

Israel passed through two stages: brought out from Egypt, and brought into Canaan. If you want to know the difference between the life you have been leading and the life you now want to lead, look at the wilderness and Canaan. In the wilderness, there is wandering; in Canaan, there is perfect rest. In the wilderness, there is want; in Canaan, there is plenty. In the wilderness, they had no victory; in Canaan, they went from victory to victory.

15

The Holy Spirit is spoken of in connection with power many times. He is not so much spoken of in connection with the graces, yet these are always more important than the gifts of power. The true marks of the kingdom are holiness, meekness, and loving-kindness.

The word "lamb" must mean to us not only a sacrifice, the shedding of blood, but also the meekness of God, incarnate on earth, represented in the meekness and gentleness of a little lamb.

16

It is good to be saved from the sins of stealing, murdering, and every other evil; but a man needs above all to be saved from what is the root of all sin, his self-will and his pride.

If the windows of your room were closed, the sun would be on the outside of the building, streaming against the shutters, but it could not enter. Take the shutters off the windows, and the light can come in and fill the room. In the same way, Jesus and His light, Jesus and His humility, are around you on every side, longing to enter into your heart.

17

Christians do not know how much they rob Christ in reading so much of the literature of the world. They are often so occupied with their newspapers that the Bible gets a very small place. Bring this noble power of a mind that can think heavenly, eternal, and infinite things, and lay it at the feet of Jesus.

The church of Christ suffers more today from trusting in intellect, in sagacity, in culture, and in mental refinement than from almost anything else. The spirit of the world comes in and leads men to try to help the Gospel through their own wisdom and knowledge. Then they rob the Gospel of its crucifixion mark.

18

I see divine things but cannot reach them. The self-life is like an invisible plate glass. We are willing, we are striving, and yet we are holding back something. We are afraid to give up everything to God.

Your heart is too holy to have it filled with business. Let the business be in the head and under the feet. But, let Christ have the whole heart, and He will keep the whole life.

The Holy Spirit could pray a hundredfold more in us if we were only conscious of our ignorance, because we would then feel our dependence on Him.

19

The smith puts his rod of iron into the fire. If he leaves it there only a short time, it does not become red hot. If he takes time and leaves the rod in the fire, the whole iron will become red hot with the heat that is in the fire. So, if we are to get the fire of God's holiness and love and power, we must take more time with God in fellowship.

Ah, the blessedness of saying, "God and I!" But I find in the Bible something still more precious. It is, "God and not I," not God first and I second. God is all, and I am nothing.

20

We often speak of the wonderful revelation of the Father's heart in His welcome to the prodigal son, but we have a revelation of the Father's love far more wonderful in what He says to the elder son: *"Son, thou art ever with me, and all that I have is thine"* (Luke 15:31). What was the cause of the terrible difference between the heart of the Father and the experience of the son? Unbelief.

If we are to experience a deepening of spiritual life, we need to discover clearly what the spiritual life is that God would have us live and to ask whether we are living that life. And if we are not living this life, we need to find out what is hindering our living it fully.

21

Unbelief is the mother of disobedience and all other sins and shortcomings: my temper, my pride, my unloving nature, and my worldliness. Though these differ in nature and form, they all come from the one root, namely, that we do not believe in the freedom and fullness of the divine gift of the Holy Spirit to dwell in us and strengthen us and fill us with the life and grace of God all the day long.

The majority of Christians seem to regard all of the Spirit's work as confined to conviction and conversion. They hardly know that He came to dwell in our hearts and there reveal God in us.

22

Walk like Christ, and you will always abide near Christ. The presence of Christ invites you to come and have unbroken fellowship with Him.

To walk through all the circumstances and temptations of life is exactly like Peter's walking on the water—you have no solid ground under your feet, but you have the Word of God to rest on.

I remember the time in my spiritual life that when I failed my only thought was to reproach and condemn myself. I found it did not do me any good. I have learned from Peter's walking on the water that my work is, the very moment I fail, to say "Jesus, Master, help me." The very moment I say that, Jesus does help me.

23

A father never sends his child away with the thought that he does not care if his child knows that he loves him. He longs to have his child believe that he has the light of his father's countenance upon him all day. If it is like this with an earthly father, how is it with God? Does He not want every child of His to know that he is constantly living in the light of His countenance?

What gift is Jesus asking you to give Him today to lead you to see what is lacking in your spiritual life? He said to the woman of Samaria, *"Give me"* (John 4:7) because He wanted to say, *"I shall give* [you]*"* (John 4:14).

24

The terrible history of mankind can never be understood rightly until we allow Scripture to teach us that there is a purpose in God that overrules all. Likewise, there is, on the other hand, an organized system and kingdom that holds rule over men amid what appears to be nothing but a natural growth and development. This kingdom keeps men in darkness and uses them in its war against the kingdom of God's Son.

25

When Christ came to save men, before He entered His public ministry, first He had to meet God and deal with Him. In His baptism, He entered into fellowship with sinners and gave Himself to fulfill all righteousness. In the vision of the opened heaven and the descending dove, as in the voice of the Father, He received the seal of the divine approval. He then had to meet the Tempter, through whom Adam had fallen. Only then could He begin His ministry among men. As definitely as Christ had to deal with God and with man in the work of salvation, He had to deal with Satan, too. There was no salvation possible unless Satan's power was acknowledged, met, and overthrown.

26

Is it possible that our lack of Christ's poverty is the cause of our lack of His riches? Is it not necessary that we not only think of the one side, *"For your sakes he became poor"* (2 Cor. 8:9), but also think of the other, *"For* [His sake] *I have suffered the loss of all things"* (Phil. 3:8)?

27

The poverty of Christ has been the assurance to tens of thousands that He could feel for them. There is also assurance in that, even for Him, earthly need was to be the occasion of heavenly help and the school for a life of faith. For Christ, the experience of God's faithfulness was the path to heavenly riches.

28

As sin entered the world with the fruit that was good for food and pleasant to the eye, so the great power of the world over men is in the cares, possessions, and enjoyments of this life. Christ came to win the world back to God. He did so by refusing every temptation to accept its gifts or seek its aid. The poverty of Christ was one of the chief elements of this protest against the worldly spirit's self-pleasing and trust in the visible.

29

Christ overcame the world. He did so first in the temptations by which its prince sought to ensnare Him; then and through that, in its power over us.

In Paul's wonderful life, as in his writings, he proved how there is much weight given to the testimony concerning eternal things when the witness can appeal to his own experience of the infinite satisfaction that the unseen riches can give.

30

In monastic days, men expected from poverty what only the Spirit of Christ, revealing Himself in poverty, could accomplish. This was the failure. Christ separated for Himself a band of men who were to live with Him in closest fellowship, in entire conformity to His life, and under His immediate training. These three conditions were indispensable for them to receive the Holy Spirit and for them to be true witnesses to Him and the life that He had lived and would impart to men.

October

October

1

After a sermon or a conversation, a soul has a little light but speedily loses it again. The soul does not still keep the promises anew before it in order to guard them so that unbelief might not again obtain the upper hand.

The question must be continually repeated, "What does God require me to believe?" In the face of whatever weakness, the answer must be at the Lord's feet: "Lord, I believe, I will believe."

Martha did not yet believe everything, but what she believed, she spoke out before the Lord. She believed in Him as the Son of the Living God. This was the principal thing and the source of greater faith. She was diligent in prayer so that her faith would be strengthened and become capable of receiving still more and more.

2

He, who knows that there is a Spirit to put faith into action, knows also that man may, with spirit and hope, strive to exercise faith. The more fully the soul believes, the clearer the revelation of the Spirit becomes. The more fully the Spirit works in the soul, the more the soul grows in the life of faith and confidence. Thus we may have the Spirit of faith.

No sooner is faith cultivated in a one-sided fashion, without a growing conscientiousness of the casting off of little sins and the sanctification of the whole heart and walk, than it becomes a work merely of the understanding or the feeling.

3

In the things of this world, we often teach our little children to utter words that they do not yet fully understand. We do this in sure confidence that the thoughts and feelings expressed in these words will gradually be imprinted on their hearts. Likewise, we constantly see idle and sinful words, which at the outset are uttered carelessly, become rooted in the heart of the speaker and bear their own fruits.

We may also observe something similar in prayer. The person who is constantly uttering the words, *"Thy will be done"* (Matt. 6:10), even though his heart does not yet fully assent to them, will be cleansed of an unwilling and antagonistic disposition simply by using the expression.

4

Sincerity is that attitude of the soul by authority of which we present ourselves to the Lord just as we are, neither better nor worse.

The Word has not defined how deeply one must feel sin before one may come to Jesus. It has no fixed measure. The first sense of need must bring us to Him. Remaining apart from Jesus is just the way to make the sense of sin less.

5

The closer we are to the light, the more visible the impurity is. The nearer we are to the Holy One, the stronger the sense of unworthiness is. The more blessed with grace we are, the deeper the conviction of sin is.

You wound Him in the most tender point when you doubt if His grace is indeed for you, and so you doubt its greatness and trustworthiness. Because you fear your own unfaithfulness, you must place your confidence in God's faithfulness.

6

It is not my business to be anxious and to say how God's Word can be fulfilled. The Lord will see to it.

If the Lord has given no promises for you, then it cannot be your duty to believe. But, as surely as the Word says, "Believe," there is also a promise that you must believe.

No lost one is so far lost that Jesus cannot find him and cannot save him.

7

Give yourself to the Lord Jesus just as you are. Do not give yourself as an offering that is worthy of Him, or as one who is already His friend. No, surrender yourself to Him as one who is dead, whom He has to make alive, as an enemy whom He must forgive.

With someone, it may be a trial in the physical life; with another, trial in the family; with another, vexation of soul; with still more, hidden conflicts with sin. But there must be trial, for as long as the flesh has everything agreeable, the soul will never wholly and with power cleave to the Lord.

8

When the Lord is to lead a soul to great faith, He leaves its prayers unheard. So it was with the Canaanite woman (Matt. 15:22–28). He answered her not one word, and when He did at length reply to her, the answer was still more unfavorable than His silence. This is always the way. If the answer came immediately, His gifts would occupy the soul's attention so much so that it would overlook the Lord Himself. It must first stand upon its Lord and what He has provided, without any answer. The Lord and His Word are to be sufficient for it.

9

The more you simply take the Word, the sooner you will feel constrained to say, "It is true. God says it. I must believe it." You must read and read again the message of God and contemplate all the promises with which God has made it sure that the Savior is for every sinner.

Water always seeks and fills the lowest place. In the same way, the moment that God finds someone abased and empty, His glory and power flow in to exalt and to bless. *"He that humbleth himself"*—that must be our one care—*"shall be exalted"* (Luke 14:11)—that is God's care. By His mighty power and in His great love, He will do it.

10

In believing, the soul wholly forgets itself and looks to God with undivided energy and hears Him. In thanksgiving, the soul must be entirely occupied with the adoration of the Godhead, the contemplation of His goodness, and the consideration of His ways. Accordingly, the more the mind is exercised in this work and is taken up with the thought of all of this, the more fixed and rooted its conviction will be that the Lord is truly a God on whom it must rely. If thanksgiving, the express mention of His omnipotence, His love, His faithfulness, and His perfection, will fill the soul, the result must be that the soul will allow itself to be concentrated on God. He who has but a single word of such a God to build upon has enough.

There must be a continual repetition of the act of faith, cleaving fast to the Word of God, until He bestows the blessing.

11

If you are still unconverted, thank Him that you are not yet in hell.

Praising and believing are one.

You also will be born again by the Living Word and be cleansed from your sin. It does not lie in you, or even in the Word itself, but in the faithfulness of God, who has said: *"He that believeth...shall not be* [ashamed]*"* (1 Pet. 2:6).

Paul always spoke of the works of the law, James of the works of faith. The works of the law are done by the personal power of man to fulfill the law of God in order to merit His favor. The works of faith are done for the confirmation and the perfecting of faith out of the power that God gives. The works of faith are not done to merit anything.

12

He who continues day by day in the use of the Word with faithful perseverance, even when he does not at once gain a blessing from it, will experience an increase of faith. It may be unobserved and slow, yet it will certainly and surely arrive. Many are often content in the morning with the general reading of the Word in the household, apart from private meditation with prayer. The reading of a chapter once a day is, as a rule, not sufficient. No, let all who truly desire to increase their faith see to it that they endeavor in the morning hour to gather manna for the day on which to ruminate. He who goes out in the morning without nutrients comes home weary in the evening with hardly any desire to eat. He who does not in the morning first lay up the Word in his heart is not to be surprised if the world assumes the first and the chief place in his heart, for he has neglected the only means of being ahead of the world.

13

Readiness and ability for any work is not given before the work but only through the work. Thus, we receive these things only after we begin to work. The child who learns to run begins before he can readily do it, and he learns in the effort. God gives commands for which we previously have had no power. Yet, He requires obedience with full right, because when we set ourselves toward obedience, strength will be given along with this initial activity.

14

Whenever the Devil is bent on keeping back anyone from salvation, he merely has to keep him back also from faith (Luke 8:12). The heart cannot at the same time move toward God and away from God, and it cannot equally desire the Word and sin. When one remembers how superficially the Word is read, what little pain is taken to understand the Word and to take into the heart and keep there every day that which should be fitted to strengthen faith, one feels how lightly and easily the Word is taken away. It costs the Devil little trouble.

15

Even the Devil knows that where the Word dwells in the heart, there faith comes. The Evil One retreats before that Word, as he did before the *"It is written"* (Matt. 4:4) that came out of Jesus' mouth. With and by that Word, the Lord God and His Spirit come to the soul.

The Lord who gives the Word will also give the faith to receive it. He who has given the promise will also bestow the fulfillment. Put yourself in the position to believe in the following with joyful confidence: It is given. Let every experience of failure, of unbelieving, of insensibility, convince you how unfortunate it would be if you had to believe of yourself. How blessed it is that you may look to God for it!

16

Humility is not something that we bring to God or that He bestows. It is simply the sense of entire nothingness, which comes when we see how truly God is all, and in which we make way for God to be all.

"Blessed are the poor in spirit: for theirs is the kingdom of heaven....Blessed are the meek: for they

shall inherit the earth" (Matt. 5:3, 5). The kingdom comes to the poor who have nothing in themselves. The earth will be for the meek, who seek nothing in themselves. The blessings of heaven and earth are for the lowly.

17

No outward instructions, not even of Christ Himself; no argument, however convincing; no sense of the beauty of humility, however deep; no personal resolve or effort, however sincere and earnest, can cast out the devil of pride. Nothing can avail but the following: that the new nature in its divine humility be revealed in power to take the place of the old, to become our very nature as truly as the old ever was.

18

The only humility that is really ours is not that which we try to show before God in prayer, but that which we carry with us and carry out in our ordinary conduct. The insignificance of daily life is the importance and the test of eternity, because it proves what really is the attitude that possesses us. It is in our most unguarded moments that we really show and see what we are. To know the humble man, to know how he behaves, you must follow him in the common course of daily life.

19

The believer is often in danger of aiming at and rejoicing in the bolder virtues: joy, contempt of the world, zeal, and self-sacrifice. Even the old Stoics practiced these, while the deeper, more divine graces are scarcely thought of or valued. These graces are those that Jesus first taught on earth because He brought them from heaven: poverty of spirit, meekness, humility, and lowliness. They are more distinctly connected with His Cross and the death of self.

20

It is the soul in which God the Creator, as the All of man in his nothingness, and in which God the Redeemer in His grace, as the All of the sinner in his sinfulness, is waited for and trusted and worshipped. The soul then finds itself so filled with His presence that there is no place for self. *"The haughtiness of men shall be bowed down, and the LORD alone shall be exalted in that day"* (Isa. 2:11).

21

Pride makes faith impossible. *"How can ye believe, which receive honour one of another?"* (John 5:44). Faith and humility are at the foundation one. We can never have more of true faith than we have of true humility. We may indeed have a strong intellectual conviction of the truth, but pride turns the living faith that has power with God into an impossibility.

There are two cases in which Jesus spoke of a great faith. Had not the centurion—at whose faith Jesus marveled, saying, *"I have not found so great faith, no, not in Israel"* (Matt. 8:10)—spoken, *"I am not worthy that thou shouldst come under my roof"* (v. 8)? Had not the mother—to whom He spoke, *"Woman, great is thy faith"* (Matt. 15:28)—accepted the name of dog and said, *"Truth, Lord: yet the dogs eat of the crumbs"* (v. 27)?

22

All God's dealings with man are characterized by two stages. The first is preparation, when command and promise train men for a higher stage. The second is fulfillment, when faith inherits the promise and enjoys what it had so often struggled for in vain. God, who had been the Beginning before man rightly knew Him or fully understood what His purpose was, is longed for and welcomed as the End, the All in All.

23

Humility suits us as creatures, as sinners, and as saints. First, we see it in the heavenly hosts, unfallen man, and Jesus as Son of Man. Second, our fallen state appeals to us and points out the only way through which we can return to our right place as creatures. Third, we have the mystery of grace, which teaches us that as we lose ourselves in the overwhelming greatness of redeeming love, humility becomes to us the consummation of everlasting blessedness and adoration.

24

What is Jesus' incarnation except His heavenly humility, His emptying Himself and becoming man? What is His life on earth but humility, His taking the form of a servant? What is His atonement but humility? *"He humbled himself, and became obedient unto death"* (Phil. 2:8). What is His ascension but humility exalted to the throne and crowned with glory? *"He humbled himself....Wherefore God also hath highly exalted him"* (vv. 8–9).

Only humility leads to perfect death. Only death leads to perfect humility. Humility and death are in their very nature one. Humility is the end, and in death the fruit is ripened to perfection. The Christian's life always bears the twofold mark. In true humility, its roots are striking deep into the grave of Jesus, the death to sin and self. Its head is lifted up in resurrected power to heaven where Jesus is.

25

We know the law of human nature: acts produce habits, habits produce dispositions, dispositions form the will, and the rightly formed will is character. It is the same in the work of grace.

It is only in the possession of God that I lose myself. It is in the height and breadth and glory of the sunshine that the littleness of the speck of dust playing in its beams is seen. In the same way, humility is taking our place in God's presence to be nothing but a speck of dust dwelling in the sunshine of His love.

26

Let us ask whether we regard a reproof, just or unjust; a reproach from friend or enemy; an injury, trouble, or difficulty into which others bring us, as above all an opportunity of proving how Jesus is all to us, how our own pleasure and honor are nothing. It is indeed blessed, and the deep happiness of heaven, to be so free from self that whatever is said of us or done to us is lost and swallowed up in the thought that Jesus is all.

27

While abiding in Christ, everything is yielded to the power of His life in us so that it may exercise its sanctifying influence even on ordinary wishes and desires. His Holy Spirit breathes through our whole beings, and our desires, as the breathings of the divine life, are in conformity with the divine will and are fulfilled. Abiding in Christ renews and sanctifies the will. Then we can ask what we want in accordance with our new will, and it will be given to us.

28

The peace of Christ is not something that He puts into your heart and that you must keep so that it may keep you. If the peace of God is to rule in my heart, it is because the God of Peace Himself is there. Can you separate the light of the sun from the sun? You cannot have the peace of Christ apart from Christ.

29

In Revelation we read of only two churches in which there was nothing to blame. In each of the others you find the word "repent." There could be no overcoming and receiving of a blessing unless they repented. Let us repent on behalf of the church of Christ, and God will make us feel how much our own sins are part of the trouble. Then God will give His Holy Spirit and will encourage us to feel that He will revive His work.

30

Every man acts always according to the idea he has of his state. A king acts like a king if he is conscious of his kingship. In this way, I cannot live the life of a true believer unless I am conscious every day that I am dead in Christ. *"He died unto sin"* (Rom. 6:10). I am united with Him, and I am dead to sin.

31

Joseph was sold by his brothers, but he saw God in it and was content. Christ was betrayed by Judas, condemned by Caiaphas, and given over to execution by Pilate, but in it all Christ saw God and was content.

All that Potiphar had, he left in Joseph's hands. Potiphar could now do the king's business with two hands and an undivided heart. Will you leave all in Jesus' hands and so be free to attend to the King's business? Every temptation will bring you a blessing if Jesus has charge of everything.

November

November

1

As each seed bears fruit after its kind and of its very own nature, and the fruit in its turn again becomes a seed, so the Spirit of Christ was the hidden seed of which the Cross was the fruit. And the Cross again became the seed of which the Spirit is the fruit. And, once again, the Spirit in the believer, and the church as a whole, is the seed of which the conformity to the Cross and the death of Christ is the fruit. It is the great work of the Spirit to fill the world with this blessed seed. It reproduces the image and the likeness of the crucified Lord everywhere. The highest work of the Spirit is to reveal the Cross, which is the wisdom and the power of God.

2

It is as the church proves itself to be the very body of the Lord Jesus, by showing forth the very same life there was in Him, that His power as Head can freely flow through her. It is as her determination not to know anything but *"Jesus Christ, and him crucified"* (1 Cor. 2:2) is seen in her being crucified with Christ, being crucified to the world, that His resurrection, joy, and power can be manifested in her. In the church, the world must hear and see Jesus Christ and Him crucified.

Intense devotion to the Cross and the crucified Lord, which leads a believer to conform to Him both inwardly and outwardly, is the first requisite of the gospel minister, if Paul is to be seen as a model for imitation. It was the one secret of his ministry and his power.

3

The confidence with which the preacher speaks does not rest on a message or a book alone. This alone can never enable him to speak as one who knows and witnesses. His commission is a living one. He can testify in power of what the Cross is and does in such measure as the Holy Spirit has revealed the Cross to him and in him. The mystery of God is *"Christ in* [us], *the hope of glory"* (Col. 1:27). This is not a thought, but a life with its knowledge, not that of the mind, but of the renewed spirit. The preacher can speak the mystery with authority when he knows that the office of God the Holy Spirit is to give the mystery entrance into the heart, however dark. The word of divine authority and power brings men into God's presence, awakens a sense of want and desire, and inspires faith in an unseen but present deliverance.

4

The Cross is the greatest of all mysteries; it is their sum and center. In it we see the mystery of the triune God: the Father ordaining the Cross, the Son bearing the Cross, and the Spirit revealing and honoring it. We also see the mystery of man: his sin, rejecting Christ; his curse, Christ forsaken of God; his worth, God's Son dying for him. Another is the mystery of love: God offering Himself to bear the sin and the suffering of man and making man one with Himself. The mystery of death and of life: death reigning, death conquered and made the gateway of eternal life. The mystery of redemption: the Cross with its sin and shame made the power that conquers the sinner and, while it humbles and slays, that wakens his hope and highest enthusiasm. There is also the mystery of God's wisdom casting down reason and filling the heart with the light of God and eternity.

5

Just as I cannot by any possibility know the taste or nourishing power of a food except by partaking of it, so there is no way of knowing Christ Jesus and Him crucified except by receiving Him into my life and being made a partaker of the disposition that animated His life and His Cross. Jesus Christ is the revelation of the life of God as it appears and acts in human nature. In the Holy Spirit, Jesus Christ has come from heaven to live and act in His disciples. We only know Jesus Christ as far as we partake of His nature and life and Spirit.

Is it any wonder that the preaching of the Gospel is not more effectual when men forget that they are preaching a divine mystery to those whom *"the god of this world hath blinded"* (2 Cor. 4:4)? The darkness of heart is a supernatural one. The power that can enlighten us is not the force of reason or argument, nor the persuasion of culture or appeal, but the supernatural enlightening and quickening of the Holy Spirit. It is God who has *"shined in our hearts, to give the light of the knowledge of the glory of God in the face of Jesus Christ"* (v. 6). The light of God shining in the heart can alone bear witness to the mystery of His love in the Cross. The great hindrance to the preaching of the Cross is a worldly spirit. The worldly spirit proves itself in nothing so much as in its wisdom, which is its chief boast.

6

Have we not often sought, by earnest thought, to enter more deeply into the significance of the Cross? Have we not, as we got a glimpse of some aspect of its glory, gone from book to book to find out what it really means? Have not some given up hope that words like *"I am crucified with Christ"* (Gal. 2:20), *"the world is crucified unto me"* (Gal. 6:14), *"baptized into his death"* (Rom. 6:3), *"dead indeed unto sin, but alive unto God through Jesus Christ"* (v. 11) should ever become truly intelligible and helpful? Is not the reason for all this that we want to grasp the hidden wisdom of God with our little minds and forget that the Holy Spirit wants to give it into our hearts and our inner lives in a way and in a power that exceeds knowledge?

The Cross brings to each one who believes in it the death that is the gate of life. The fullness and the power of the Spirit are given through it.

7

Remember that His Holy Spirit, His crucifixion spirit, is in you. It is not in you to give you clear or beautiful thoughts, which might delude you, but to communicate the very temper and disposition out of which the Cross grew.

When the church has to complain of the with-
holding of the saving power, the reason must be that
the crucifixion spirit, in which the saving power
finds its life, is wanting. It must be because the
church is not saying, as Paul said, *"I...came not with
excellency of speech or of wisdom, declaring unto you
the testimony of God. For I determined not to know
any thing...save Jesus Christ, and him crucified"* (1
Cor. 2:1–2).

In that life of our Lord, the most remarkable
thing, its great feature, its divine mystery and glory,
was His being crucified on the cross. He proved how
life has no purpose except to be made to serve God's
will. He also proved how suffering and sacrificing all
is the highest and most well-pleasing religion and
obedience, and how there is no way out of life into
the glory of God, except through dying to it.

The Cross means the sacrifice of all. To know
the Crucified in the conformity of His death, we
need to *"count all things but loss"* (Phil. 3:8). The
Cross demands our lives. A ministry does not come
in excellency of speech or wisdom, but it boasts in
the weakness and the foolishness of the Cross. This
will convict the world of its sin and its earthliness,
and will lift men up to a supernatural life.

8

We must always return to our Lord, and men
like His servant Paul, and see what the elements are
that make up the crucifixion spirit. These elements
include the following: a deep sense of the sinfulness
of sin and of the righteousness of God's judgment on
it; an entire separation from the world, and a clear
protest against its defection from God under the

power of the god of this world; a lifelong surrender of our own will and pleasure as a sacrifice to God to work out His will in us; a parting with all excellency of speech and wisdom that make the Cross of no effect; a passion of love for the souls of men, giving life up completely for them as Christ did; and the acceptance of death to all that is of human nature, which is sinful and under the curse, so that the life and power of heaven may work all in us. This was the spirit that animated Paul as it animated Jesus Christ.

9

Heartily accept your sense of ignorance. Depend entirely on the Spirit to reveal the hidden mystery *"in the hidden part"* (Ps. 51:6). Count confidently on the work He is doing in you. Keep your heart set on your crucified Lord in meditation and worship, with an increasing sense of how little you know or understand, and the blessed Spirit will do His hidden work where you cannot see it. Trust Him fully, and He will do it.

The Cross is the wisdom of God in a mystery, and the Spirit of God alone can reveal it. How this truth would teach us how to preach the Cross correctly! A mystery must be accepted on authority. The apostle or preacher holds a divine commission to tell men in the name of God what they do not know and what they cannot understand, until they first bow before God to accept it.

10

The spirit of the world, apparently honoring and proclaiming the Cross, is the great reason why the church's preaching is so little in demonstration and in power (1 Cor. 2:4). It robs the Cross of what its chief glory is, that it is the wisdom of God in a mystery, with the Holy Spirit from heaven as its only interpreter.

The sense of mystery is of the very essence of true worship. Though at first it burdens and bows down, it soon becomes like the high mountain air in which faith breathes freely and strongly. The sense of mystery brings the soul under the power of the Invisible and Eternal, the Holy and Divine.

The Cross is the wisdom of God in a mystery. Let us bow and worship and wait in deep humility. What God devised, God will reveal. We have come to Mount Zion, and the Lamb is the light of it. As we adore what we cannot and would not understand, the Spirit will impart what God has bestowed. And we will learn to walk as men who know that God is working out in them who love Him what ear has not heard and what heart cannot conceive.

11

Let anyone who desires to be brought into fellowship with his crucified Lord hold fast to the words, *"The wisdom of God in a mystery....God hath revealed* [it] *unto us by his Spirit"* (1 Cor. 2:7, 10). As you gaze on the Cross and long for conformity to Him, do not be weary or fearful because you cannot express in words what you seek. Ask Him to plant the Cross in your heart. Believe in Him, the Crucified and now Living One, to dwell within you and breathe His own mind there. It is not the work of Christ alone, but the living Christ Himself as the Crucified One whom the

Gospel reveals. A sinner often wearies himself in vain in trying to take hold of the work of Christ and its blessings. When he sees that it is Jesus Christ Himself, and Him crucified, he has to trust. He finds One who takes charge and works all in him.

12

How much your life depends on your relation to the promises. Connect the promises with the Promiser, the Promiser with His unchanging faithfulness as God, and your hope will become a glorying in God through Jesus Christ our Lord.

Confession strengthens hope. What we utter becomes more real to us. It glorifies God. It helps and encourages those around us. Fullness of faith and fullness of hope make the heart true. Because we have nothing in ourselves, and God is to be all and to do all, our whole attitude should look up to Him, expecting and receiving what He is to do. The entrance into the Holy of Holies is given to us as priests, there to be filled with the Spirit and the love of Christ, and to go out and bring Christ's blood to others.

No effort of your will can bring forth love. It must be given to you from above.

13

The knowledge of what Christ has won for me—the entrance into the heavenlies—and the work He did to win it—the shedding of His blood—is very precious. But there is something better still, and that is that the living, loving Son of God is there personally to make me a partaker of all the blessedness that God has for me.

In the court there were the brazen altar and the laver. At the former, the priest sprinkled the blood, and at the latter, he washed before he entered the Holy Place. At the installation of the Passover, they both were first washed and then sprinkled with blood. In the great Day of Atonement, the high priest had to wash before he entered the Holiest. The Word and water are joined together (see Ephesians 5:26; John 13:10; 15:3), because the Word is the external manifestation of what must rule our whole outer lives. The liberty of access, the cleansing that the blood gives, can only be enjoyed in a life in which every action is cleansed by the Word.

14

Nothing will help us to keep ourselves unspotted in this world except the Spirit that was in Christ that looked upon His body as being prepared by God for His service. It is for every man, as it is for the Master, to put away sin by the sacrifice of self. What delights God is not burnt sacrifices, but the sacrifice of our own will to do God's will.

Our eating and drinking, our sleeping, our clothing, our labor and relaxation, all influence our spiritual lives. They often interrupt the fellowship we seek to maintain. Through the body, Satan conquered in Paradise; in the body, he tempted Christ. Christ was perfected in the sufferings of the body.

15

Where God is, there is heaven; the heaven of His presence includes this earth, too. Faith makes us one with Christ. By faith the soul can enter into the Holy of Holies, into the light of God's holy presence

and love, and into full union with Him. By faith the
soul can abide continually, because Jesus abides continually.

The boldness to enter into the Holy of Holies is
not a conscious feeling of confidence; it is the objective, God-given right of entrance of which the blood
assured us. The measure of our boldness is the
worth God attaches to the blood of Jesus.

Which is now greater in your sight: your sin or
the blood of Jesus? There can be only one answer. As
your sin has until now kept you back, let the blood
now bring you closer and give you the power to
abide. The blood has put away the thought of sin
from God, and He forever remembers it no more.
The blood has also put away the thought of sin in
me, the evil conscience that condemns me. The better things that the blood speaks in heaven, it speaks
in my heart, too.

16

The truth of Jesus' heavenly priesthood is so
often powerless because we look upon it as an external, distant thing, a work going on in heaven above
us. The one cure is to know that our Great Priest
over the house of God—and we are His house, too—
is the glorified Jesus who makes His presence and
power in heaven by the Holy Spirit to be as real
within us here as it is above us there.

There are seasons for Bible reading, prayer, and
churchgoing. But how speedily and naturally the
heart turns to worldly things. It is not the worship of
a true heart. God asks the affection and the will. The

head and the heart are in partnership, but the heart must lead. Our religion has been too much of the head, or intellect: hearing, reading, thinking. The Bible never says draw near with a clear head, but it says with a true heart.

17

The surrender of all becomes possible only when the soul sees how truly Jesus engages to put His own delight in God's law into the heart, to give the will and the strength to live in all God's will.

Faith accepts the promise in its divine reality. Hope goes forward to examine and rejoice in the treasures that faith has accepted. Faith will perhaps be most tried when God wants most to bless. Hope is the daughter of faith, the messenger it sends out to see what is to come. It is hope that becomes the strength and support of faith.

18

One chief cause why some do not grow more in grace is that they do not take time to converse with the Lord in secret. Christians, give yourselves, give your Lord, time to transfer His heavenly thoughts to your inner, spiritual life. Take time to remain before Him until He has made His Word living and powerful in your souls. Then it becomes the life and power of your life.

Books can become a blessing to the reader only when they always bring him to that portion of God's Word covered by the book, in order that he may meditate further upon it himself and receive it for himself as from the mouth of God.

19

Only one word was necessary to find food for angels. But to prepare for man a banquet upon this accursed earth, a banquet of heavenly food, this cost God much. It cost nothing less than the life and blood of His Son, to take away the curse and open up to them the right and the access to heavenly blessings.

The greater the work is that a man undertakes, the more important the preparation is. Four days before the Passover, the Israelite had to make his preparations. The Lord Jesus also desired that care should be taken to obtain an upper room, furnished and ready, where the Passover might be prepared. When I am called on to meet my God and to sit down at His table, I will see to it that I do not approach it unprepared.

20

Great thoughts of Jesus and large expectations of what His love will do will set the heart aglow and be the best preparation for meeting Him. To have a deep-rooted renunciation of myself, in order to be willing to live through Jesus alone, is the attitude of a soul that leads to a blessed observance of the Last Supper.

Even as the little weak infant who does not know how to eat is fed by his mother's hand, so will Jesus break for me the bread of heaven and impart to me what I need.

21

There is nothing on earth that awakens love and rouses it to activity so powerfully as the thought of being desired and loved. Jesus' desire is toward me. Believe and ponder this wonderful thought until you feel drawn with overmastering force to give yourself over to Jesus for the satisfaction of His desire toward you. Then you will be satisfied, too.

22

The more the believer really despairs of himself, the more glorious Christ will become in his eyes. The more keenly he feels every sin, the more Jesus will become to him. Every sin is a need that calls for Jesus. By the confession of sin, you point out to Him the spot where you are wounded and where He must exhibit the healing power of His blood. Every sin that you confess is an acknowledgment of something that Jesus must cast out and the place that He is bound to fill up with one of the lovely gifts of His holiness. Every sin that you confess is a new reason why you should believe more and ask more, and a new reason why Jesus should bless you.

The very same light that enables you to feel the curse of sin more deeply enables you also to discern the perfect and final victory over it. The experience of being utterly lost prepares the way for the experience of being utterly redeemed.

23

The *sin offering,* by which atonement was made, was the type of the sacrifice of Christ alone. *"He hath made him to be sin for us"* (2 Cor. 5:21). The *burnt offering,* which had to be wholly consumed by fire on the altar, as a symbol of entire devotedness to the service of God, was the same type of sacrifice as that of Christ and of the sacrifice of believers, in which they surrender themselves to the Lord. The idea of offering thanks is exhibited fully through the feast of *thank offering* and in the fellowship that ensues.

24

The priests might eat of the sin offering by which atonement was made as a token of their fellowship with God through the Atonement. The Lord's Supper is our fellowship in the perfect sacrifice of Jesus Christ, which has done away with sin forever. Of the thank offering, in which dedication to God was shown forth, the offerer himself might also eat, in recognition of his fellowship with God in this dedication. The Lord's Supper is a communion with Christ, not only because He offered Himself up for us, but also because, in and with Him, we offer ourselves to the Father with all that we have.

My Savior, come into me. My faith can only be the fruit of what You give me to know of Yourself.

25

He loves us so dearly that He greatly values our love. Our love is to Him His happiness and joy. He requires it from us with a holy strictness. So truly has the eternal Love chosen us, that it longs to live in our remembrance every day. You know, Lord, it is not by any force that my heart can be taught to remember You.

If by Your love You dwell in me, thinking of You becomes a joy—there is no effort or trouble, but the sweetest rest.

When I hear the glad tidings that Christ died for sin, I obtain courage to say, "Sin is mine, and Christ, who died for sin, died also for me." When I first look on sin, I can boldly say that Christ is mine. The forgiveness of sin is, as it were, the pledge of entrance into the whole riches of the grace of God.

26

All knowledge of the truth, and all acquaintance with the Gospel, are of no avail without personally taking hold of that short phrase, "For me." And that word of man has, on the other hand, its foundation in the word of Jesus, "For you."

As by the circulation of the blood every member of our body is kept unceasingly in the most vital connection with the others, so the body of Christ can increase and become strong only when, in the loving fellowship of the Spirit and of love, the life of the Head can flow unhindered from member to member.

27

To be thankful for what I have received, and for what my Lord has prepared, is the surest way to receive more. A joyful, thankful Christian shows that God can make those who serve Him truly happy. He stirs up others to praise God along with him. If my Savior went singing from the Lord's Table to the conflict in Gethsemane, may I, in the joy of His redemption, follow Him with thanksgiving into every conflict to which He calls me. The nearer to the throne of God, the more thanksgiving there is. In heaven they praise God day and night. A Lord's

Supper, pervaded by the spirit of thanksgiving, is a foretaste of it.

28

Life must be fed with life. In wheat, the life of nature is hid, and we enjoy the power of that life in bread. It was to make heavenly life accessible to us that the Son of God died like the seed in the earth, so that His body was broken like the bread grain. It is to communicate this life to us, and to make it our own, that He gives Himself to us in the Last Supper.

29

"I have meat to eat that ye know not of" (John 4:32). Jesus had a hidden manna that He received from the Father, and that was the secret of His wonderful power. Jesus received the nourishment of His life from God in heaven. The doing of God's will was for Jesus the bread of heaven, and since I have now received Jesus Himself as my heavenly bread, He teaches me to eat what He Himself ate. He teaches me to do the will of God.

When Abraham returned from the campaign for the deliverance of Lot, Melchizedek, the priest of the Most High God, set before him bread and wine (Gen. 14:18). *"To him that overcometh"* (Rev. 2:7), says Jesus, "to him who works and strives and overcomes, I will give the hidden manna for him to eat." Heavenly food brings heavenly strength, and heavenly strength brings heavenly work.

30

It is one of the characteristics of God's work, that with Him the end is as certain as the beginning.

He has sought me and made me His own. What He
has thus done to me points back to what He did for
me: He gave His own Son, and by His blood He
bought me for Himself as His own possession. And
that again points back to eternity. He chose me and
loved me before the foundation of the world. My
soul, ponder what this means: He has begun (Phil.
1:6). Then you will be able joyfully to exclaim, *"the
LORD will perfect that which concerneth me"* (Ps.
138:8).

December

December

1

It is when parents love the Lord their God with all their heart and strength, that human love for their children will be strengthened and sanctified. It is only to parents who are willing to live really consecrated lives, entirely given up to God, that the promise and the blessing can fully come true.

An angel of the Lord had appeared to Manoah's wife to predict the birth of Samson. This angel's name was Wonderful. This is still the name of the parent's God.

2

Not only does the child call forth the love of your heart because of his tenderness and lovingness, but his waywardness and willfulness call for it still more, since they put it to the test and teach it forbearance and gentleness.

Children who are allowed to be unruly and self-willed will speedily lose their childlike faith. What is said of men—that they have wrecked their faith because they have thrust from them good consciences—holds true of children, too.

3

Now with the Bible of God's grace, and then with the books of God's glory in nature, the whole day, and the whole life, is to be an uninterrupted fellowship with the Holy One. It should consist of the continued and spontaneous outpouring of the heart in the language of life, to prove that God's presence and love are a reality and a delight. This is the source:

> *Thou shalt love the LORD thy God with all thine heart....And these words, which I command thee this day, shall be in thine heart: and thou shalt teach them diligently unto thy children, and shalt talk of them when thou sittest in thine house, and when thou walkest by the way, and when thou liest down, and when thou risest up.* (Deut. 6:5–7)

4

Many parents never understand the truth that to train for God's service secures the fullest salvation. God says of Abraham: *"I know him, that he will command his children...and they shall keep the way of the LORD"* (Gen. 18:19). Remember Pharaoh's words: *"Go ye, serve the LORD...let your little ones also go with you"* (Exod. 10:24).

5

The secret of home rule is self rule, first being ourselves what we want our children to be. A calm stillness of soul that seeks to be guided by God's Spirit is one of the first conditions of success in our own spiritual life. The same is true of the sacred influence we wish to exert on our children.

6

Of old, God sought above everything to train His saints to be men of faith. Faith is the soul's surrender to God. It begins with faith in His Word. In an age of doubt and questioning, teach your child to accept what he or she cannot understand, even what appears mysterious and contrary to reason, because God, who is wise and great, has said it. The child wants to trust, the Word wants to be trusted, so let your earnest faith bring them into contact.

7

Christ's healing work is spoken of as the natural result of His atoning work, of which Isaiah had spoken as a way of bearing our sickness (Isa. 53:5). (See Matthew 8.) He left, among the exceedingly great and precious promises that are the riches of His church, the assurance that *"the prayer of faith* [would] *save the sick"* (James 5:15). He has a thousand times over led His children by His Spirit—applying the promise of His doing whatever we want if we abide in Him—to believe and receive the healing of a sick child.

8

Mother, God gives you this picture of Elizabeth and her child of promise: *"Thou shalt have joy and gladness; and many shall rejoice at his birth. For he shall be great in the sight of the Lord"* (Luke 1:14–15). These verses talk about three marks of a child born under the covering of the Holy Spirit. Among men, such a child may not make a name; in gifts and talents he may not be great, but he will be great in the sight of Him who does not see as man sees. He will be a vessel God can use for His work, one who truly prepares the way for the coming of the Lord in His kingdom.

9

"Weep not; she is not dead, but sleepeth" (Luke 8:52). Jesus draws near the lifeless form of each little one, over whom a mother's heart is weeping. He reminds the mother that death has been conquered and that the loved one is not dead, in the terrible meaning that sin gave that word. He reminds her that, truly, the child sleeps in that deep and blessed sense, which the word that He speaks now has. There is a better life than the life of this earth; it is the eternal life in which God dwells. He took this little one so that He might draw you heavenward, so that He might empty your heart to make more room for Himself, and so that you might be drawn to Him in your need and be prepared to receive the new revelation He has to give of His power, His love, Himself, and your life.

10

The Syrophenician woman believed and triumphed with one weapon: more prayer, more trust (Mark 7:25–30). Mother, pleading for your prodigal child, you have her example and a thousand words of promise and a revelation of the Father's will and the Savior's power and love, such as she never had. In the face of all doubts, claim the promise of an answer to prayer in the name of Jesus. Yield yourself to the Holy Spirit, to have everything brought to the light that you must cast out. Do not trust the wrestling urgency of your petition, but seek your strength in God's promise and faithfulness, in His power and love.

11

It is as parents serve God on the Sabbath that the first condition will be fulfilled for teaching their children to love it. In the beauty of holiness, and as the spirit of holiness breathes on and from them, in the services of the Sabbath, the parents will serve God and act as examples to their children. Since that day is not a day of strict observance to the parents, but one of joyful worship and delight, of real, loving fellowship with God, the children will learn to love the Sabbath.

12

God's highest gift to creation was His will, that man might choose the will of his God. Obedience is the path to liberty. Parents often say that to develop the will of the child, the will must be left free. The will of the child is not free, but passion and prejudice, selfishness and ignorance, seek to influence the child in the wrong direction. Your highest work is to be God's minister in leading your child's will back to His service. To know how to refuse the evil and choose the good will be to choose Christ and holiness and eternal life.

13

It is because the Christian parent does not realize that ruling his house well is a simple matter of duty, a command that must be obeyed, that so many children are ruined by parental weakness.

Not to restrain the child is to dishonor God by honoring the child more than God, because the duty God has imposed is made to give way to the child's will.

14

"Only believe" (Mark 5:36). Living faith will teach us to see new beauty and preciousness in our children. It will awaken in us a new earnestness and desire in everything to hold and to train them for God alone. The name, "Faith Home," has been appropriated to certain special institutions, and we will boldly claim it as the name of our own dear home, because everything is done in the faith of Jesus.

15

God asks and expects us to copy Him in every way when doing our work as parents. God's fatherhood is our model and study. In the tenderness and patience and self-sacrifice of divine love, in the firmness and righteousness of divine rule, the parent will find the secret of successful training. In a Christian father, a child ought to have a better exposition than the best sermon can give of the love and care of the Heavenly Father and all the blessing and joy He wants to bestow.

16

The one likeness between Adam and his seed was disobedience. The one resemblance between Christ and His seed is obedience. *"Whosoever shall do the will of my Father...is my brother, and sister, and mother"* (Matt. 12:50). The link in a family is a family likeness and a common life shared by all. The bond between us and Christ is that He and we together do the will of God.

17

The branch is a perfect likeness of the vine. The only difference is, the one is great and strong and the source of strength, and the other is little and feeble, always needing and receiving strength. In the same way, the believer is the perfect likeness of Christ.

How can we glorify God? We cannot do so by adding to His glory or bringing Him any new glory. In a vine bearing much fruit, the owner is glorified, as it tells of his skill and care. In the disciple who bears much fruit, the Father is glorified. Before men and angels, proof is given of the glory of God's grace and power. God's glory shines out through such a disciple.

18

We ask how much a man gives; Christ asks how much he keeps. We ask what does a man own; Christ asks how does he use it. The world thinks more about the money getting; Christ thinks about the money giving. The world looks at the money and its amount; Christ looks at the man and his motive. We look at the gift; Christ asks, "Was the gift a sacrifice?"

19

Asking the following would be the spirit of the world in the church: "If our Lord wanted us to give Him all, like the poor widow who cast her farthing into the treasury, why did He not leave a clear command?" In looking at what we give, we need to look at our giving all. We must put all at His feet, as the spontaneous expression of a love that cannot help giving, and gives just because it loves.

20

If we could only see the Lord Jesus in charge of the heavenly mint, stamping every true gift and then using it for the kingdom, surely our money would begin to shine with a new luster. We would begin to say, "The less I can spend on myself, and the more on my Lord, the richer I am." Day by day, give as God blesses and as He asks—it will help to bring heaven nearer to you, and you nearer to heaven.

21

One of the ways of manifesting and maintaining the crucifixion of the flesh is never to use money to gratify it. The way to conquer every temptation to gratify the flesh is to have the heart filled with large thoughts of the spiritual power of money.

How many count themselves really generous, because of what they *will*, while what they *do*, even up to their present means, is not what God would love to see.

22

When you lie down at night, weary, the bed holds you up and allows you to stretch out your whole body and to rest there. God, the Everlasting

One, stretches out His arms and says, "Now, soul, come and rest." He will take you up individually. The Father is very near. He is not a general father and God of the universe, but a special Father for every child of His.

23

Do you believe that if God had sent an angel to whisper every moment in your ear, "The Everlasting God is keeping you," you would then have understood how you were to be kept? You have something better than an angel. God has actually given His Holy Spirit into your hearts to keep you always in remembrance of the presence of Jesus. Through the remembrance of His presence, you will be kept trusting Him every minute.

24

The experience of the love and the saving power of our incarnate, crucified, glorified Lord depends entirely on His indwelling us to reveal His presence and to do His work. The Lord Jesus brings the heart that accepts and trusts Him to dwell within into sympathy and harmony with Himself. He becomes your life. He will live in you, and all your thoughts, tempers, dispositions, and actions will have His life and Spirit breathing in them.

25

Jesus was born twice. The birth at Bethlehem was a birth into a life of weakness. The second time, He was born from the grave: *"the firstborn from the dead"* (Col. 1:18). Because He gave up His first life that He had by His first birth, God gave Him the life of the second birth, in the glory of heaven and on the throne of God.

Jesus' heart toward us is all love. His work was, and is nothing but, the revelation of infinite love and tenderness. Nothing but love on our part can be the proof that we have really accepted and known His love.

26

To do God's will, Christ came from heaven. To do God's will in you, He has entered your heart. God gave us a will, that with it we might intelligently will what He wills.

When Christ comes in to take possession, He will, by His Spirit within, make you what God wants you to be: comformable to the image of His Son. Christ's life is altogether too high and too divine for us to reproduce. It is His own life, and only His, but He will live it out in us.

27

The childlike disposition of loving subjection is the true fulfilling of the law, not what a man does or brings, though it may be the performance of the law. The worth of our religion depends wholly on our relationship to God.

In the midst of all a little child's working and praying, he always has the hidden sense of his mother's nearness. The Christian can become so closely knit to his God, that in the midst of the toilsome activities of earth, there may always remain the blessed feeling, "My God sees me, and I can look up unto Him."

28

The joy of forgiveness will not always remain, unless it is confirmed as the joy of sanctification. When the first joy begins to yield, many a Christian has ascribed the loss to God, saying it is a trial that He has sent him. If the Christian had only asked for grace, not only to be washed from guilt, but also to be liberated from the dominion of sin, he would have found that with the progressive work of grace in the soul, a progressive joy would have been ministered to him by God.

29

The more you cleave to God and commit yourself to His Word and counsel, the more steadfastly you will stand. Let the Word be your food. Strive by it to think what God thinks, to will what He wills. If the Word of God is thus the rock of your confidence, you will only be moved as little as there is variableness, or shadow of turning, with God.

30

The law of God guards the entrance to the gate of heaven. It will let no one within who is not whiter than the snow. *"Wash me, and I shall be whiter than snow"* (Ps. 51:7). God has offered us nothing less than this; nothing less than this can bring us full peace. Alas, how many are seeking peace in their own activities, endeavors, and experiences, but they cannot find the stable, full peace that Jesus gives and *"which passeth all understanding"* (Phil. 4:7).

31

God offers us the book of Psalms as a prayer book, adapted to our needs, because the prayers come from His Spirit and are therefore divine. Yet, they are just as genuinely human, because they come from those who are flesh and blood and are in everything like ourselves. When children learn the ABCs, the teacher puts the sounds into their mouths. In the Psalms, the Lord God puts into our mouths the very words with which we may come to Him.